How to Start and Run
Your Own Bed & Breakfast Inn

Ripley Hotch
&
Carl A. Glassman

STACKPOLE
BOOKS

Published by
STACKPOLE BOOKS
Cameron and Kelker Streets
P.O. Box 1831
Harrisburg, PA 17105

Printed in the United States of America

Cover photo by Marilyn Stouffer
Cover design by Tracy Patterson

First Edition

10 9 8 7 6 5 4 3 2 1

Library of Congress Cataloging-in-Publication Data

Hotch, Ripley
    How to start and run your own bed & breakfast inn / Ripley Hotch and Carl Glassman. — 1st ed.
        p.   cm.
    Includes index.
    ISBN 0-8117-2441-7 : $14.95
    1. Bed and breakfast accommodations—Management. 2. Hotel management. I. Glassman, Carl A. (Carl Averom), 1953– II. Title.
TX911.3.M27H6627   1992
647.94—dc20   92-20979
                                                                  CIP

For our partners, Owen and Dinie

Contents

Preface

How to Start and Run Your Own Bed & Breakfast is a cooperative effort. Most books with multiple authors are impersonal reportage, but this one cannot be. Our opinions are laced throughout, and we don't always agree with one another. In order to avoid confusion, "I" is the principal writer, Ripley Hotch, and "Carl" is Carl A. Glassman. This puts the responsibility for stylistic infelicities where it belongs and allows you to affix the blame for foolish opinions on whichever of us deserves it. "We" refers, therefore, to both of us or to the innkeeping profession's opinions generally (in those few cases where there is general agreement).

Ripley Hotch is co-owner of The Inn on Montford in Asheville, North Carolina, and formerly of Boydville Inn in Martinsburg, West Virginia. He is currently contributing editor for technology at *Nation's Business* magazine. He has been the editor of *Detroit* magazine, an editor for the *Florida Times-Union* in Jacksonville, and an assistant professor of English at the University of Illinois. He holds a Ph.D. in English from the University of California, Berkeley, and is the author of *How to Start a Business and Succeed.*

Carl Glassman is co-owner and veteran innkeeper at Wedgwood Collection of Historic Inns in New Hope, Pennsylvania. Since 1982 he has offered how-to workshops and consulting services to aspiring innkeepers. A licensed realtor and management consultant, he is an adjunct professor of hospitality programs at New York University. He founded and served as president of the first regional and statewide inn associations in Pennsylvania. Carl holds an M.S.W. degree in policy and planning from Rutgers University and is a frequent contributor to national inn and travel publications.

Acknowledgments

One of the great delights in writing this book has been talking to innkeepers and the professionals who serve them. Innkeepers are a special breed. Even though we approached some for interviews during their busy season, the overwhelming majority gave generously of their time and advice. How generous, only fellow innkeepers can really know. Innkeepers are constantly being asked by guests about how to get into the business, and it can be wearing.

In spite of that, our fellow innkeepers went over what is for them the old, familiar ground and did it as if for the first time. That alone reconfirms the reputation of warmth, generosity, and sharing that all travelers associate with the time-honored term *innkeeper*. We've mentioned as many of our fellow innkeepers as we could in these pages, but we have inevitably left some out where others covered the same ground. Having a number of innkeepers say the same things was important to us; it confirmed trends and general advice. So to those we didn't mention, our thanks.

Some innkeepers are simply fantastic at what they do. You'll see them quoted rather more often than others. These people are truly awesome in their generosity, energy, intelligence, foresight, and creativity. In any other profession they would be well-paid. It's a tribute to them and to this peculiar business that these innkeepers feel well-paid even when they bank very little or nothing.

So we offer a special thanks to the network of professional innkeepers, both the seasoned pros and the novices, for their enthusiastic support, encouragement, and assistance.

I have to thank two of my colleagues at *Nation's Business,* Meg Whittemore and Michael Barrier, for some interview assistance. Both are avid inn-goers. They talked with several innkeepers on their visits with our question list and brought back the results. This enriched the final product. My brother, Kim, also contributed his unique perspective from Alaska.

Carl adds thanks to the many wide-eyed aspiring innkeepers he has met through his seminars and other workshops. Most are now not only successful innkeepers, but also leaders in their state and regional associations.

A special thanks from both of us to our families, partners, and staff for covering for us during high season while we worked furiously to complete this project.

Introduction

Some professions or callings seem to have an irresistible romance to them—astronaut, painter, poet, Olympic athlete, Supreme Court justice. But for most of us, these ambitions are beyond reach. We generally settle for amateur status.

Two other romantic callings seem more in reach: owning a restaurant and being an innkeeper. An astonishing number of otherwise sane people express a desire to do these, and a surprising number give one or the other a try. This in spite of the fact that restaurants fail more often than any other business and innkeeping is notoriously low-paying. Why do people still want to try it?

The romance of our caring profession comes from a love of being on stage. Innkeeping is a form of theater in which you create the settings and star in the performance. You dream of being the perfect host with the perfect home. You assume you will be entertaining and expansive, a raconteur and guide. When guests like what you do, you get something very close to the glow performers get when they are warmly applauded. You think about the graciousness of the lifestyle and its relative freedom (working at home! no more going to an office! all that space!). Your inn is your castle, your kingdom, your baby, your profession, and your lifestyle. What could be more perfect?

Well, when something seems too good to be true, it probably is. That isn't to say that innkeeping can't be a great life, because it can. But it can also be very tough. The word most often used by innkeepers to describe their work is *confining*. And they hadn't really expected that. They are able to have everything at home; but they can't get away from it. They have to be there to answer the phone (it might be a reservation), or to take care of an arriving (or departing) guest. Maintenance and visits from inspectors and the week's baking and any number of other things limit the innkeeper's freedom.

For those who feel the draw of innkeeping, however, there is no discouraging word. Its pull can be almost overwhelming. For some of us, there is simply no way to avoid giving it a try.

You are probably one of those. In that case nothing we say will discourage you, so we won't even make the attempt. Read this book—and several others—and take some of the advice in them. You'll have a better chance of success.

Two things are essential to creating a true inn: you—the owner—must be present as a host, and you must run a business. If you're interested in a hobby, that's fine, but that's a bed & breakfast home, not an inn. If you are an absentee, then you are an owner, but not an innkeeper.

If you are about to take up innkeeping, you're going to find a lot of people willing to give you advice. That's what we're doing here. Innkeepers, however, are not always open to advice; all of us who have struggled into the business are opinionated. We often speak in absolutes, as if there were only one way to do things. We don't much like criticism either, because we have so much of ourselves invested in our businesses.

We advise you to read other books, to get more ideas and opinions, to talk to other innkeepers yourself. And we advise you to be careful about listening to people who have never kept an inn. It isn't that they don't know useful things so much as they simply do not have a sense of what is possible. Going outside the innkeeper circle is good for financial projections, for accounting, and for legal advice. But when it comes to what amenities you should offer, how to handle guests, how to create ambience, and above all how much you can do, go to the folks who have been there. They are the ones who can give you a real feel for innkeeping.

We've gathered the best information we can from innkeepers and those who serve the business—analysts, former innkeepers, insurance agents, lawyers, general business advisers—so that you can know what to do and in what order. If you follow this book almost like a recipe, then you will have a better than fighting chance to succeed.

There are other books on starting inns, but they are written either by writers who have never been innkeepers or by former innkeepers whose experience and point of view are limited to their own inns. Both these approaches are valuable. But what we are offering is advice based on interviews with many different innkeepers and service professionals. This approach will give you a real sense of the variety in this business. There are so many different ways of being successful that you should not think there is only one way of doing it right.

On the other hand, there are some standard ways of going wrong and some experiences common to all innkeepers. To succeed, there are some things that we all agree must be avoided.

You must be willing to change, if necessary, some of your most cherished plans. You may have to make some decisions and compromises you do not like. You will also have to be willing to make changes as you go along, because the world does not stay the same. This is being written in the grip of a recession, for example, and some innkeepers are feeling the pinch, but many more are expanding and succeeding because they can alter their methods to fit the circumstances.

In fact, recessions, which hurt other businesses, can be a help to inns that cater to people taking short trips. During a recession, people cut down on longer vacations and take more quick get-away holidays—the inn's specialty. Both of our inns, Wedgwood and Boydville, have significantly increased business during these hard times, so don't let the doomsayers discourage you. Circumstances do control a lot of your life, but opportunity favors those who are prepared.

This book is arranged to give you an overview of the inn-keeping business and details of the steps you should take to create a functioning business. This will allow you to enjoy being an innkeeper instead of worrying whether business has been properly taken care of.

When business *has* been taken care of, you can take the innkeeper's special pleasure in listening to guests praise your inn and your hospitality. As Owen said one cold, slow, March Sunday when we had ushered out the only guests of the week-end, "When someone likes the inn that much, it makes it all worthwhile." If you can take pleasure in such intangibles, then this may be the job for you.

1

The Inn Business

The inn business is not small. There are no certain estimates, but a good guess is that there are roughly 20,000 bed-and-breakfast inns, country inns, and homestays in the United States. Another measure is an estimate of rooms rented annually: at average rates of occupancy, approximately 15,000,000 for inns. Contrast that with the 10,000,000 rentals in 1991 for Best Western, the largest North American motel chain, with 3,300 properties.

Another measure is the number of sole proprietors. According to *American Demographics* magazine, about 10,000,000 Americans work in their own unincorporated businesses. The largest number are in services (30 percent) and the largest number of those—321,000—are in lodging places: bed-and-breakfast inns, boarding houses, trailer parks, camps, and "similar residences."

As it grows, the business is becoming more professionalized. What was a random collection of guest houses is emerging into a field that has professional associations and an increasing interest in standards. Now more than ever it is important for new innkeepers to be armed with much more information than those in the vanguard had.

The opening and maturing of the inn business was much like the settling of the Old West. It started with generally unsettled territory and a notion that something was "out there." Then came the pathfinders, the few brave souls who started letting rooms in their houses after all the tourist homes of the 1940s and 1950s were displaced by the genius of Kemmet Wilson, founder of Holiday Inns.

Then there were the pioneers, who had a better notion of what they wanted to be doing. They started the small inns that Norman Simpson first wrote about in the 1970s in *Country Inns and Back Roads*. Then came the homesteaders like Carl and Dinie in the late 1970s and the settlers like Owen and me in the mid-1980s. When Laura Ashley starts creating signature inns and when Relais et Chateaux (the international luxury chateau-country house hotel chain) expands into North America, then our business is no longer a cottage industry.

So it's a good idea to begin with a survey of what we mean by the term *inn* (a term corrupted from use by so many joints) and what the trends are in this diverse and burgeoning field.

DEFINITIONS

There's a good deal of argument—not always friendly—about the terminology used to describe inns. We'll start with the *generally* used terms, and their ordinary meanings:

Bed-and-breakfast home

Also called a *homestay* or *host home,* this is a private home, run part time by its owners for a little extra money or as a way to meet people. It is the closest to the English B&B and was the start of the whole business in the United States. Small B&B homestays can be as professionally run as any full-service inn, but they are simply homes with an extra room, where you stay cheek-by-jowl with the family. Breakfast is included and often served with the family. Homestays do not have a business sign and are generally not regulated. Their business comes through overflow referrals from inns or bookings from a reservation service. For a commission these services market and book reservations, often abiding by strict guest profiles provided by the hosts, such as "nonsmoking Christian motorcyclists" or "married couples with an interest in opera."

Bed-and-breakfast inn

This is the professionally run four- to eighteen-room inn in which the owner-innkeeper is resident on the property (or very close by) and considers herself or himself to be a professional innkeeper. There may be assistant innkeepers, but the main contact of the guest is with the owner.

Inns are usually historic or architecturally interesting buildings and are considered legitimate businesses. They have zoning
board approval, collect sales and occupancy taxes, have use and
occupancy permits, and maintain commercial insurance coverage.
Breakfast is always included, though it may be continental. B&B
inns are regulated, often quite heavily, by state and local laws.

Country inn

Also called *full-service inns* and sometimes just *inns* (surely
you didn't think we were going to make this easy), they range in
size from five to twenty rooms, and can be in the city or the
country. The country inn has a restaurant that serves meals
other than breakfast. Breakfast may not be included in the rate,
though it usually is. Because of the restaurant, and often a bar,
these are the most heavily regulated of inns.

Anything larger than about 20 rooms we regard as a small
hotel, though small hotels can be as elegant and charming as the
B&B or country inn. We believe, however, that it is not possible
for an innkeeping couple to maintain the ambience of an inn
with more than 20 guest rooms.

There may be other gradations among these categories, but
they are often less categories than niches within categories, such
as "historic inns," or "country house inns." Bernice Chesler,
one of the first guidebook authors (hers are *Bed & Breakfast in
New England* and *Bed & Breakfast in the Mid-Atlantic States)*,
is often called America's Bed & Breakfast Ambassador. She lec-
tures often and everywhere, runs promotions for the inns in her
books, and has been a careful and professional observer of the
inn business from its beginnings. She says that B&B owners are
"very sure of what they do and how they're different. But the
traveler really doesn't care about definitions. They care if you are
a home or an inn." Beyond that, you have to explain the subtleties.

Throughout this book, we are talking about B&B inns, and our
intention is to help you become an innkeeping professional.
Even if you are interested in a homestay, however, much of the
advice here is certainly going to be helpful.

TRENDS IN THE BUSINESS

The business is changing, and there are a number of trends—
some positive, some not—that any aspiring innkeeper should

be aware of. We'll come back to these in later chapters, but a quick survey of them is appropriate here.

Professionalism

"Innkeepers are becoming more professional—and that does not mean commercial," says Bernice Chesler. "We have reached the stage where it is a career for many, a primary source of income. Ten years ago, when they first started to blossom, the more common reason was for additional income and a certain lifestyle."

Cynthia La Ferle, former editor of *Innsider* magazine (unfortunately no longer published), says that more innkeepers are joining organizations intended to help them become more professional and they're going to more workshops and seminars.

One simple indication of increasing professionalism is the number of inns listed in the Yellow Pages. American Business Information, an Omaha firm that counts these listings to spot business trends, says that the number of B&Bs grew by 24 percent in 1990, to a total of 5,526. There's a big discrepancy between that and American Bed & Breakfast Association estimates of the number of inns, but clearly the number of professional inns, as opposed to homestays, has to be growing fast. If you're serious about being in business, you'll be listed in the Yellow Pages.

Confusion among hotels, motels, and inns

What is confusing to the traveler (and dangerous for the inn owner) is that many hotels and motels are calling themselves "B&Bs" and are putting in the kinds of amenities associated with inns, including an "innkeeper" who greets the guest. But that innkeeper is an employee with no stake in the business (the exception is a franchisee). We think this is confusing for travelers, who may never actually stay in an inn. It makes marketing the real B&B inn much more difficult.

More specialization in style

As the market becomes more crowded and the inn traveler more discerning, it is important for you to know what kind of inn you want and how to project that to your potential guests. Cynthia La Ferle deplores the tendency of people to "jump on a bandwagon they know nothing about. We're getting stuck in a Victorian mode; that's well and good if you have a fine building and you want it to be authentic." But there are other viable and attractive styles, she says. "Some are now doing English Tudor. Some are looking to the Arts & Crafts era, or the Mission era. Some are going with a more contemporary look. I'd like to see the trend of knowing who you are, what you've got, and going with it, not trying to be like the cute little inn down the road."

As an aspiring innkeeper you will have to think hard about the kind of inn you want. This goes beyond architecture. We have some suggestions for you in Chapter 5.

Finding new guests

Some inns are trying to appeal to the business traveler. These travelers may like the inn environment, says Cynthia La Ferle, but they need certain things like telephones in the rooms, desks, good lighting, and availability of computers and fax machines. "You can't let the trappings override the ambience, though. You could have a phone jack in the room, and a phone brought in when the traveler needs it." Or you can provide a phone booth or centrally located guest phone with a number different from the inn's general number. Either way, she says, you should decide you're going to stay true to the inn atmosphere or you're not going to try to attract the business traveler.

Sandra Soule, author of *America's Wonderful Little Hotels and Inns,* says inns should consider appealing to children. Most inns do not; many even discourage children. But, she says, they're missing a bet.

Many innkeepers are marketing to single women traveling for business and pleasure. These women often find the homelike inn environment more comfortable, safer, and less threatening than a large steel-and-glass hotel. The ambience of an inn's parlor is a welcome alternative to the cold anonymity of a hotel lobby.

The over-fifty traveler is a market niche well worth reaching. Active retirees are probably going to be the fastest-growing travel group. They have the time for and interest in smaller inns, and they often travel midweek and off season by preference. But they have their own special needs the innkeeper must be aware of.

Other niches are business meetings, weddings, banquets, and similar sorts of gatherings. But for each of these you must have an appropriate facility and a willingness to deal with special circumstances.

Inspections for quality and consistency

State and local regulatory agencies, local and regional inn groups, and travel associations are all tending toward more inspections. Among the latter, the most famous are the Mobil Travel Guide and AAA. Both have included B&B inns in their programs for some time, under slightly different requirements than they impose on larger outfits. Most recently, the American Bed & Breakfast Association (AB&BA) has instituted inspections. These inspections include a strict series of requirements and end in a ranking.

Inn groups have a more informal inspection method. Since they are often associations of neighbors, the inspections can deteriorate into backbiting. Some associations have fallen apart because of feuding. Others, like the Independent Innkeepers Association organized by Norman Simpson, have a base large enough that they can establish some standards.

There is a trend toward increased regulation by both the public and the private sectors. Public policy concerns on the state level revolve around issues of health (food service and water quality) and safety (fire and panic). Local governments are concerned about maintaining the character of a neighborhood. Through zoning ordinances they often restrict B&Bs by limiting the number of guest rooms and requiring minimum lot size and off-street parking.

Private-sector regulations focus on a different set of qualities. Insurance companies want inns to be adequately covered for business interruption, product liability, and potential losses due to fire and theft. Automobile clubs, inn associations, guidebook authors, and the AB&BA are concerned with such "soft" standards as innkeeper presence, light bulb wattage, cleanliness, and the quality of linens.

Carl recalls one memorable off-season midweek afternoon. "We had a state fire marshal inspect our inn for emergency exit signs while an AAA field inspector was investigating the adequacy of our interior window and door locks, and a potential house guest was bouncing on a bed mattress, checking its firmness! All three were 'unscheduled inspections,' of very different, yet related, aspects of our inn. We passed all three, receiving a renewal of our use permit, a three-diamond rating from AAA, and a two-night walk-in reservation by the guest."

State and local regulations are becoming more detailed and, some innkeepers would say, more onerous. The positive side of this increased regulation is that it ensures a general upgrading of quality; what is better for the business as a whole will certainly be better for individual inns. There's no question that we are all getting many first-time travelers, and one bad inn can lose a guest permanently. Regulations that prevent schlock operations from starting up (or that close some) are in everybody's interest.

On the other hand, regulations that are too picky destroy the delicate financial balance of inns. There are many observers who think that the larger motel and hotel industry would very much like to do this. That might be paranoia. Then again, it might not.

Changing attitudes to rates

Bernice Chesler once remarked, when I complained about price resistance among travelers to rates that had not changed for two years, that there are always new travelers. New travelers in the late 1980s were not particularly sensitive to price. First-time inn-goers in the early 1990s, however, seem inclined to resist rates they perceive to be too high.

Travelers in the 1990s seem to be looking for value as opposed to the luxury-at-any-price mentality that reigned in the 1980s. Private amenities—fireplaces, hot tubs, scenic views—do command higher room rates, but travelers are often looking for "affordable luxury."

The changing vacation

Gone are the days when Mom and Dad packed Fido and their 2.3 children in a big station wagon and headed west for a two-week family vacation. Family lifestyles, economics, and work realities no longer permit such travel for many people.

The U.S. Travel and Tourism Administration has statistics that reveal a general trend since 1973 for Americans to take shorter, more frequent trips closer to home. Tom Troland, marketing director of *Country Home* magazine, did a survey of travelers in 1989 that corroborated these findings.

Extended weekend travel and mid-week escapes within a one-tank drive of home now appear to be the norm. Gracious inns in historic, rural, or village settings are right on target. And as long as inns offer what many marketers call *high touch* (warmth and genuine hospitality, personal service, and attention to detail) to their guests, who live and work in an increasingly high-tech world, they will continue to grow and prosper.

Carl has noticed a corollary to this trend: the tendency of guests to "roost in one spot" and explore a region over several days. Day trips from the base might range as far as a hundred miles, from which the guests return "home" each evening.

This tendency is especially true of older travelers, who are less than pleased to have to find a different place to stay each night; worrying about whether they will like the next place as well as the last one or wishing they had stayed longer may spoil the day. Innkeepers can take advantage of this trend with clever marketing.

Upping the ante

Rating systems and coverage in upscale publications are causing the public to expect a great deal of inns, particularly those in the luxury category. Some of these expectations are spilling over onto inns that have no such pretensions, as guests come to expect amenities that are expensive to provide and, in some contexts, ridiculous.

Ray Compton of Spring Bank in Frederick, Maryland, finds this trend depressing. "People are being led to believe that they need private baths, whirlpools, fax machines, fireplaces, telephones, televisions, king-size beds, and on and on. Ours is a historic house, and I'm trying to give people a feel of the past. There's wear and tear on the furnishings, but that shows it's close to the original. People like Sarah Sonke of the AB&BA and her ratings are not helping us to find the person who likes our kind of place."

Many innkeepers actually try to discourage demanding guests from coming lest they not appreciate the experience.

This issue will be taken up in several places in this book. We suggest ways for you to create the kind of inn you want and then reach the kind of guest who will enjoy your house—without sending out false signals.

Innkeepers often create two major problems for themselves. One is the problem of honesty. Too many new innkeepers, buoyed by their enthusiasm, simply oversell. In the worst cases they lie about what they provide. This does a disservice to all other innkeepers. Heaven help you if you have done this and get a demanding guest. The unpleasantness of that experience is hard to match.

The second is a growing problem: the perception of public officials that innkeepers are likely to skirt the law whenever possible. We don't think this is true, but for reasons of expense, experience, time, and ignorance, innkeepers are sometimes unwilling to focus on the business and legal aspects of their new profession. They often keep very poor tax records or avoid getting permits.

Keep records from the beginning. If you're not good at it, then get a good bookkeeper or accountant. A certified public accountant who thinks about your business will often save more money for you than you will spend on him. Another good reason to keep good records is that the IRS is beginning to do more audits of B&B inns, on the assumption that people are hiding money that they take in. That some inns have done so, combined with the poor tax records of honest innkeepers, has reinforced that assumption (bureaucrats do not like poor records).

We'll come at both these problems in several ways as we go along. We don't think anyone is going to give you trouble if you are honest and know what laws and regulations apply to you.

More food service

More and more travelers expect to take an evening meal in the inn. We suspect that this trend will continue. Inns have a number of ways to approach this problem (or opportunity, depending on your perspective). One is to hire a chef, build a commercial kitchen, hire a wait staff, and start taking dinner reservations. This is expensive. The kitchen costs upwards of $50,000, a chef isn't cheap, and a wait staff is hard to manage. Add to that the liquor license and all the added attention from various licensing and taxing bodies, and you have a recipe for a headache.

Other inns have exceptions that allow them to serve meals on a small scale. Such arrangements are fraught with danger, however, because of insufficient insurance. And since such arrangements involve zoning exceptions and health exceptions, they could be changed at any time.

Another solution is to bring in outside caterers for specific meals. Trying food service on this scale will allow you to discover whether it is something that you want to do and whether it is profitable. Catering is a clearly defined outside service; you're not doing any of it. The problem is that this cannot be done flexibly; you don't want to absorb the cost of uneaten meals that you ordered on speculation. And if you get into this in a large way, you're still going to need waiters. You'll also be pretty tired. Still, if you want something special for guests, you can offer meals to groups of at least a certain size, guaranteed as your rooms are.

COMPARING US WITH HOTELS

"Comparisons," said Dr. Johnson, "are odious." When we compare ourselves with the hotel and motel industry, however, we aren't at as much of a disadvantage as you might think.

For one thing, the hotel-motel industry is overbuilt and over-leveraged. They borrowed too much money and built too many rooms in the 1960s. In some senses that hurts us, if guests try to put us in the same category. We ought not to try to compete with the hotel-motel industry on price for a number of reasons: it invites the wrong kind of comparison and forces us toward unprofitability.

Hotels and motels often got financing from overgenerous banks in the 1980s, and they have not adapted well to the new realities of the 1990s. Some chains have gone into bankruptcy; others have sold out. The remainder do not have occupancy rates that are significantly better than most inns.

In fact, things weren't so hot for the hotel industry even in the go-go 1980s. They ran up ten consecutive years of losses from 1981 to 1991—reaching losses of $1,000 per room for the year. (You don't really want to know where the money came from to sustain these losses, but some of it came out of our pockets.) Hotel occupancy rates dropped down to 59.2 percent in 1991.

The economy segment of the hotel-motel industry has done better. It's the fastest-growing; people are willing to cut down on frills to save money. The occupancy rates of that segment get into the 62 to 63 percent range.

What does this means for inns? 1) Our rates compare reasonably well to the industry as a whole, given that we don't have their marketing power. 2) Our guests really want to stay with us. 3) Be very, very careful about competing on price.

We are also much less leveraged; the full service hotel-motel industry is being eaten alive by its debt service, because so many units were built. Over time, as the industry shakes out and there is less lending for lodging, the number of rooms will shrink, occupancy rates will go up, and we'll still be in fine shape in the inn business.

COMPETITION AMONG OURSELVES

It is probably inevitable that as inns grow more attractive as an alternative to the nine-to-five job, more people will be trying it than should. It just looks too easy. Arna Fay, who owns the Fox Creek Bed & Breakfast in Fox, Alaska, puts it succinctly; "Everyone in this area with an extra bedroom seems to think they can open a B&B, charge half what the hotels charge, brew up coffee in the morning, throw a couple of rolls on the table, and make lots of money. Greed and ignorance are creeping into the business."

This is a serious matter. A good part of the charm of this business has been the generosity of long-time innkeepers toward newcomers. Not only have many established innkeepers been willing to do seminars (whose price never covers the value given), but they also offer advice without charge as new innkeepers struggle with the inevitable bumps in the road.

There are, however, exceptions to this rule. If it comes to a choice between saving the business and generosity to the innkeepers, the business is going to come first. At some point, overbuilding is going to strain nerves. In New England, for example, the early 1990s have seen a severe recession following on an overbuilt and overpriced inn market. That some inns will fail is inevitable.

If into that market come predators—people who trade on the businesses of those who do things right—then there will be a general decline in the ability of all of us to offer first-rate accommodations at a rate that will pay.

Other nasty practices we have seen: guest-stealing (referring guests when you are full, but keeping their names and calling back if you have a cancellation); misrepresenting other inns; calling government agencies or regulatory groups such as AAA with anonymous accusations of law-breaking in other inns.

People do strange things when they get desperate. We hope we can prevent some of these things from happening to the business by urging you to have a strong financial foundation, to do good research, to present a unique inn, and to operate ethically.

2

Beginning at the Beginning

"PREDICTABLE PERSONS WORK FOR WAGES; UNPREDICTABLE
PERSONS ARE INNKEEPERS."
                                    —Hugh Lineberger

Certainly it's true that innkeepers are unconventional. Heinz
Haibach of the Millstone Inn in Cashiers, North Carolina, says
"Of course, you have to be a little bit crazy to do this."

Dick Butkus, innkeeper with his wife, Ellen, of Hollileif in
Wrightsville, Pennsylvania, described us all very well after a
year of innkeeping, "A wonderful quality of innkeepers is that
they are all, at least a bit, out of step with the world. A great
attraction of innkeeping is the ability to make one's own decisions and choices. For the most part, innkeepers are fun-loving,
cheerful people. Perhaps the eccentricity of the innkeeper is
what makes each B&B a special place. A little craziness can go a
long way in making a weekend memorable."

WHO SHOULD BE AN INNKEEPER

Early on in our research for this book, Carl, Dinie, and I were sitting at the breakfast table of the Scarlett House in Kennett
Square, Pennsylvania, after innkeeper Susan Ascosi had served
us breakfast. We were speculating about who made a successful
innkeeper, not in terms of the business end of things, but rather

in terms of who really enjoyed the experience. Susan had been a nurse and an administrator, I had been a teacher, and Carl and Dinie were both in human services.

We talked about other innkeepers we knew and came to the conclusion (since confirmed by many interviews) that the good innkeepers had been in service professions, and often care-giving ones. Nurses (not doctors), salespeople, teachers, consultants (who are teachers of a sort), homemakers, personnel professionals, and so on seem to have what it takes to deal with guests.

Innkeepers seem to come in pairs (the sole innkeeper is fairly unusual), and the two partners complement each other in interesting ways. If one is a caring type, the other will often be a business type. One will be the maintenance person, the other the marketer. Or various characteristics of the two will combine in unusual ways—but ways that work.

Sid and Judy Clemmer moved from Texas to Leadville, Colorado, to open the Leadville Country Inn in 1989. Judy had worked for more than seven years as the director of a day-care center with 87 children and 15 staff people. Sid had worked as a salesperson for his father (a Coca-Cola bottler) for years. Even though each thought Judy would deal more with the people side of innkeeping, it has worked out the other way.

John and Maureen Magee of Rabbit Hill in Lower Waterford, Vermont, are a classic example. John was in life insurance and Maureen was a teacher and administrator. "But," Maureen says, "John was a teacher before he was in life insurance. In our careers and in life, we were serving people. We can now recognize that we love to take care of people." Taking care of people for an innkeeper means showing a kind of care that will surprise the guest. "We have aspiring innkeepers who come to us for advice, and we ask them why they want to do this. Some never mention the guests and never mention giving of themselves. But we need to ask ourselves continually what differentiates the hospitality we offer from that of a hotel or motel. That owner is not likely to sit in the emergency room with the guest who fell and broke an arm. We try to find the little unspoken thing that a guest needs and meet that need. A person who is continually coughing in the dining room might find a hot toddy or hot tea in the bedroom, and some Halls cough drops." Hugh Lineberger opened the Gastonian in Savannah, after a 22-year career in temporary personnel work. Although his wife, Roberta, worked for a time in their agency, she was mostly a homemaker, raising five daughters. The Linebergers were over sixty when they opened the Gastonian from scratch.

Hugh says that most innkeepers are older people. "Older people are more interested in love than money." He thinks of himself as a salesman. "It used to be a common saying in Savannah that if you shook hands with Hugh Lineberger, you had a brochure on the backswing. We sell all the time; that's what life is, it's selling."

The owners of Old Yacht Club Inn, Santa Barbara, were in education. Nancy Donaldson was a dean and Lu Caruso was an assistant principal. One day Nancy came into Lu's office and said, "I'm sick and tired of chasing these kids around in my high heels. I have better things to do."

Says Lu, "Nancy had done extensive traveling in Europe and always stayed in bed-and-breakfasts. She found this house and said the worst thing that could happen, if it didn't go, was that we would have an interest in a beautiful house near the ocean in Santa Barbara and enough rooms to accommodate all of us. So we said okay and gave it a whirl." Eventual success followed.

Nancie and Lee Cabana took over Brookview Manor in Canadensis, Pennsylvania, in July 1991. Lee had been an executive with the Red Cross and Nancie was a recreational therapist. As new innkeepers in the Pocono Mountains, they quickly learned not to bowl over houseguests with their old credentials or job status. "From a guest's perspective," says Lee, "there are only two roles at an inn: the server and the servee. A good innkeeper appreciates that guests may not give a damn about his M.A. in English. They just want help in getting their luggage upstairs. Coming from the human services made the transition into the hospitality industry very easy for us."

People in these professions at least understand that they can deal with people and like it. These successful innkeepers come back again and again to what all of us who have done this know: You have to be able to be around people all the time. "If you love to have houseguests every day, seven days a week, and if you love to talk, repeating worn-out stories and answering nonsensical questions, then inns are for you," says Hugh Lineberger.

If you have not been in a people profession, at least do some soul-searching. As Bernice Chesler says, "You will be associating with other people absolutely full-time. And for the successful innkeepers, that is one of the perks. They really do love people. The friends they make through the business are a major reward, one they were seeking in their previous profession, and never found."

It seems, in fact, that most innkeeping partnerships have one member who was miserable, or at least unfulfilled, at the work he had before. That's the negative that pushes them into innkeeping, the other side of the love of people that pulls them into innkeeping.

THE WAYS OF BECOMING AN INNKEEPER

There are three principal ways of becoming an innkeeper: get hired as one, buy a going inn, or start an inn from scratch.

Arline Stephan, former resident innkeeper at Wedgwood, is a good example of the professional staffer. She says she had all the motivations to be an innkeeper, "except that my husband had no interest in innkeeping, and neither of us had a strong desire to be self-employed." So she set out on a national job search and landed her position, in a place she likes and in an area where her husband could find work in his field.

For years Annette King has been an inn-sitter and consultant for inns from North Carolina to California to Rhode Island. She says that she has no interest in the headaches of owning an inn, but she loves being an innkeeper. So although she hasn't the potential profit from ownership, neither does she have the burden of finding the money to keep one going.

King's Cottage, a seven-room B&B in Lancaster, Pennsylvania, employs a full-time nonresident innkeeper to provide support to owner Karen Owens. "Since my husband, Jim, is still employed full-time outside the inn," Karen says, "I definitely need professional staff to properly run my inn. And the staff can hold down the fort when we take our vacation."

We think that more innkeeping positions will open up as successful inns expand and as the industry matures. Though not for everyone, working at an inn does have its advantages. As Arline says, "Because I review the incoming mail, I process the reservation deposit checks—but I give all the bills to Carl and Dinie. This is one small example of enjoying the fun parts of innkeeping without the hassles of ownership."

The changing nature of the inn business makes our suggestions about becoming an owner now different from the ones we might have given five or ten years ago. When Carl started in 1981 there were not that many inns. When I started in 1987 there were enough for it to be considered a strong trend. Now there are so many that new inns have to work much harder to be noticed. And if you're not noticed, you'll never make it.

In a later chapter, we'll go into the details of both buying an operating inn and starting one from scratch; for now, we want to look at why you would choose one approach or the other. It's the most basic of your decisions—even before you decide you're going to be an innkeeper, because that one you can rescind up until the time you sign the closing papers.

If you start from nothing, many more of your decisions are going to be critical. You will have a great deal of work making sure that your licenses are going to be correct (or that you can get them at all). You will save the money of paying for a going business, but you will have to do much more work to assure there will be a business for you. Are you willing to be a pioneer in a new area? Do you have the stamina for writing (or rewriting) laws, working with contractors, lawyers, accountants and others who have never dealt with inns, and finding the market—if there is one? (For more on this, look at Chapter 5.)

If you buy another inn, you have to deal with the previous clientele, which may not be the one you want. That was the case for John and Maureen Magee, who bought Rabbit Hill Inn as an ongoing enterprise. "We made our peace with the fact that part of the price was the existing clientele," says Maureen. "It was a family place, inexpensive and European plan, and we just gave that up."

Carl and Dinie bought a former rooming house and turned it into the Wedgwood Inn. They felt that having an already going business, even though a different one, was a help to them. When Sid and Judy Clemmer bought the Leadville Country Inn, it had been closed for a while, but they knew their licenses would be in place.

Owen and I started Boydville from scratch; there wasn't even another inn in town to serve as a guide. We were the first with *everything,* and what we saved by not buying a previous business, we spent in agony and aggravation.

You *can* start from scratch with less hassle: Deb and Gary Leitner of Hillside Farm in Lancaster, Pennsylvania, had a large farmhouse with the potential for four to six guest rooms, two acres of grounds, a quiet rural setting and a strong tourist area. They attended an innkeeping seminar, visited other inns, and in Gary had an important resource: an electrical engineer. He could do all of the conversion work himself. They both kept their full-time jobs so they could ease their way into innkeeping gradually.

Money and location can do wonders. Hugh and Roberta Lineberger started the Gastonian from scratch; they insist they wouldn't do it any other way. But they spent a great deal of money—over two million dollars—and have a great location in Savannah.

Inheriting a piece of property or an old house is a good way to start—if you can arrange it. Dan and Darlene McNeill inherited the Inn on Providence in Charlotte, so it made sense for them to start their inn there. They made a great success of it. Now Charlotte has refused to allow new inns in the city limits unless they are grandfathered. Although this is shortsighted of the city, it gives the Inn on Providence a great advantage.

As more innkeepers retire from the business and commercial lenders become more restrictive, leasing a working inn will become a real option. The McNeills decided to leave innkeeping and put their property on the market. Joann Celani, who had opened an inn on her farm in Romeo, north of Detroit, wanted to buy it (her husband was ready to retire from the cold weather).

"It takes too long to start from scratch, so I wanted to buy an established one," says Joann. But the Michigan property did not sell, so Joann worked out a lease arrangement with the McNeills. "The only thing that was strange was walking into someone else's home. I felt like an intruder."

But, she says, it was just the thing to do. In Romeo, the farm was out in the country and didn't do much more than pay the insurance and provide a little spending money. "In Charlotte, we were paying our lease, and paying our daughter (who was the assistant innkeeper), and we had cleaning help—*and* I was making money.

"Buying a going proposition is the way to do it. All the licenses
are in place, the brochures are done, you have a good reputation,
you're in the books. Leasing is marvelous; what better way to
find out if you like it?"

Joann wasn't able to sell the property in Michigan and decided
not to keep the lease at the Inn on Providence after a year. The
McNeills started back into innkeeping and decided not to lease
again. Sometimes, especially when the real estate market is
slow, leasing options will be more available. When the market
is tight, however, this won't be true.

Leasing is not often an available solution, but you might find
it is just the one for you. Eventually you may be able to demonstrate to a bank that the property is doing well enough for you to
finance the purchase out of earnings. For younger people without
a large nest egg, this may be the way into innkeeping.

There are other, often complex, methods that can make
innkeepers out of people with less credit or means. But these
require the advice of professionals (real estate agents, lawyers,
accountants, and bankers). Don't give up when conventional
routes don't get you there. If you really want an inn, there are
ways, and people to help you find those ways.

WHAT YOU NEED BESIDES MONEY

Money is an obvious necessity for inn owners. We'll save
money matters for Chapter 4, but you should know that it exists
in many forms and can be made to go a long way.

There's another extremely important asset, besides good
humor, for potential innkeepers: good health. As an innkeeper,
you really are indispensable (ask innkeeping pairs how life is
when one of them is too sick to move). If you are prone to illnesses
or have a debilitating condition, don't consider innkeeping.

Likewise, if you are not energetic and self-starting, stay away
from this business. You should be the kind of person about
whom others say, "I don't see how you do all the things you do."
For most innkeepers, 17-hour days are routine. And they are
hard days, full of physical activity, mental gymnastics, and psychological strain.

As Dane Wells, owner and innkeeper of one of the best-
known inns, the Queen Victoria in Cape May, New Jersey, says,
"If you do it on a professional level, you're going to be working

a seventeen-hour day, and you're going to be doing it seven days a week. You have to have a little streak of workaholism going through you to survive."

Innkeepers typically think they can do everything. Often they can. Here's a sample of recommended innkeeping skills: light carpentry, gardening, troubleshooting problems of old houses, using a computer, writing press releases, handling Chamber of Commerce committee work. All this in addition to being a congenial host, of course. If you can do all this, you certainly have the skills to own an inn.

The mistake we all make is to assume that we can do it all *at once.* Time really is unforgiving, so you should also be the kind of person who knows where the limits are.

That's easy advice to give. When Carl and Dinie decided to renovate the third building in the Wedgwood Collection of Historic Inns, the Aaron Burr House, Carl put in 18 to 20 hours a day on the renovation. A week after opening the inn, Carl contracted double pneumonia. Everyone who has been involved in a renovation project has pushed the limits, and that's okay once in a while, but you can't make a habit of it.

3

If You Don't Do Anything Else . . .

"THE MOST CRITICAL PIECE OF ADVICE THAT ANYBODY
NEEDS IS TO UNDERSTAND THAT THE BED-AND-BREAKFAST
BUSINESS IS A BUSINESS."

—Murray Burns

We've spent a lot of time asking successful innkeepers what
they did to ensure their success and what they would have done
differently if they had it to do over. Surprisingly few said they
would have changed their approach. But some rules emerged
that you should take to heart. These rules won't keep you from
failing, but they will form a safety net.

The rules are centered around taking care with details before
you take the final step. You need to do as much advance planning as you can, because all hell breaks loose when you walk in
the front door and take possession of your inn property. Some of
the rules we'll look at in detail here, and others we will take up
in more detail in later chapters.

RULE 1: FIND A GOOD LOCATION
The most important rule in innkeeping is having a good location.
How you define "good" in part depends on the kind of inn you
want to have and the kind of innkeeper you want to be.

There are certain locations that offer good opportunities for inns: college towns, many national parks, major historic sites, mid-sized business destination cities, and getaway locations like seashores and mountains. Not many places have all these qualities, and those that do are pretty well saturated. Each of these kinds of locations imposes different characteristics on inns located there.

College towns, for example, will put you in the room-rental business, and price will be a major consideration. You will have parents visiting their kids, parents bringing kids to look at the school, football fans, concert-goers and performers, visiting faculty and lecturers, recruiters, and so on. Most of these people will be there for a specific purpose, and they will be looking for convenience at a reasonable price. Relaxation is usually not their goal.

National parks and *historic sites* will bring you travelers interested in history and touring. These will often be older guests, with plenty of discretionary income. They will be looking for special advice on how best to see the sights they have come for. Innkeepers will need to be knowledgeable about the logistics for visiting the local attractions. Williamsburg, St. Augustine, and Gettysburg are all principal historic locations.

Newport, Rhode Island, is a typical coastal area with dramatic scenery and has the added attraction of historic sites. It is so popular that it has more than a hundred B&Bs and homestays. Yet during the tourist season (four months of the year) every room in every establishment may be filled.

The Voss Inn is located in Bozeman, Montana, near Yellowstone Park. Innkeeper Bruce Muller says, "Yellowstone draws visitors from every state in the union, plus many guests from other nations. I think we have to know more about Yellowstone than the park rangers! Guests particularly like our driving instructions. We direct them on back roads through small towns to get there."

Favored *recreational locations* are oceans, lakes, and mountains. Bicycling is becoming a popular yuppie pursuit and, in addition to boating, skiing, and hiking, draws visitors to these areas. These outdoorsy people are looking for more rustic kind of inns as a rule, so if you plan to open an elegant place filled with porcelain and lace, avoid Vail.

Mary Davies' Ten Inverness Way in Inverness, California, is a four-room inn located in a great hiking area near Point Reyes National Seashore. A veteran innkeeper since 1980, Mary says,

"I like my guests to feel comfortable walking into the inn without first having to take off their hiking boots. I'm not a froufrou person and haven't decorated the inn that way. Most of our guests come to this area for outdoor activities and they aren't froufrou people either. We keep on hand maps of the park and materials on bird watching, horseback riding, and hiking trails. The books we sell in the living room also reflect these interests. We tend not to attract couples looking for a romantic escape."

One major trend among travelers is to take shorter vacations closer to home. The *weekend getaway* and its companion *midweek escape* have become popular with harried city workers. Some areas have become tourist meccas; within a few hours' drive of major cities, they make excellent getaways. Galena, Illinois, just three hours from Chicago or Milwaukee, is such a place. So is the Upper Peninsula and Mackinaw Island in Michigan. Bucks County in Pennsylvania is another popular getaway destination. Its location within four hours of one-third of the U.S. population makes it a great home for inns.

Urban escapees are often younger couples without children. These college-educated professionals look for upscale inns in country or village settings.

Galena is the location of Aldrich Guest House, an elegant Greek Revival house that offers five bedrooms. A Chicago native, innkeeper Judy Green left a New York City publishing career in 1985 to purchase the then-one-year-old fledgling B&B. The inn is her sole means of support and she operates it seven days a week year-round with only cleaning help and an occasional innsitter. Over 50 percent of her business is urban dwellers.

"I can usually spot a city couple by the car they're driving—often a late model, two-door sports car," Judy says. "They are often seeking a romantic spot, or simply a place to relax from the stress of their corporate jobs. When they make reservations, they are happy to hear we don't have in-room telephones or televisions, and they are absolutely delighted that we have lace-canopied beds and bathrooms with pull-chain commodes and claw-foot tubs.

"They often take in some historic sightseeing and antique-hunting and usually ask about reservations at the best restaurants. This is definitely a quality-conscious market, not a cost-conscious one."

Such areas can be very tough for aspiring innkeepers who plan to start from scratch, because acquisition costs may be high and those areas may be approaching saturation. They may also be at the mercy of gasoline prices (and availability), since most guests reach their getaway destination by car, not public transportation. If a getaway destination is reliant on one metropolitan area for most of its guests, the inn's business may be adversely affected by a regional economic recession.

If you find a developing destination of this kind, it can be a real opportunity *if* you have the financial resources to hold on while it matures. One problem for such areas is getting mid-week business. Boydville, for example, is located in a developing getaway location, near two national historic parks, a good deal of recreation, and shopping. All the inns in our area have difficulty getting midweek business, though most have no problems on Saturday nights. Obviously, filling all your rooms one night a week is never going to get you to 65 percent occupancy.

The U.S. Travel and Tourism Agency found recently that shopping has come to be a significant form of entertainment. Outlet malls will be attractive to many guests, not as the primary draw for your inn, but as one of many things to do in the area.

Business travelers have discovered inns and are filling them during the week. That makes *mid-sized cities* like Charlotte, San Diego, or Minneapolis, good potential locations. Such cities often have restrictive zoning, however, limiting inns to historic areas or to a maximum of two rooms, which dooms a serious professional innkeeper. They also have the opposite problem of tourist destinations: how to fill on weekends.

Urban inns often have an entirely different clientele with very specific needs. They usually attract single business people who require convenient locations for doing business. If a getaway inn provides R&R (romance and relaxation), an urban inn must provide T&T (telephones and televisions).

Kathleen Williams operates the 18-room Society Hill Government House in Baltimore. "Private baths and in-room telephones and TVs are essential if you're going to serve the corporate traveler," she says. "Inn policies must be different, too. You must accept a variety of credit cards for payment, and check-in policies must be very flexible—business travel is canceled or changed frequently. And since business guests often travel by airplane, they arrive and check out at all hours of the day and night!" This, of course, affects an inn's staffing patterns.

Inns located in business destination cities may also have to provide conference rooms and meeting arrangements for their guests. The Richmond Hill Inn in Asheville, North Carolina, is an 1889 Victorian mansion offering 12 guest rooms with private baths and in-room phones and TV. The owners also recently renovated the inn, making it handicap-accessible, upgrading the kitchen, and adding a conference room.

Innkeeper Danny Wimer says, "We wanted to aggressively pursue *business* business, so we made the physical changes necessary to do so, including the addition of fax services. We also had to get licensed to serve meals other than breakfast to our corporate guests. We made significant capital improvements and a substantial investment here."

The nine-room Loveland Inn in Loveland, Colorado, added a new meeting and reception center by purchasing another building across the street. The owners, Bob and Marilyn Wiltgen, renovated the new property with the sole purpose of adding space for executive sessions and banquets—for as many as 66 people.

Business travelers may be conscious of costs. Inns often have to meet or beat the room rates of downtown hotels and motels. Anne Hillestad, innkeeper at the ten-room Queen Anne Inn in Denver, says, "We're located four blocks from the central business district. We do a lot of work with business people. To stay competitive, we offer them a corporate rate Sunday through Thursday nights."

"Urban innkeepers need to be flexible," says Dick Jones, innkeeper with his wife, Mary, of Chelsea Station, a five-room two-story brick Federal Colonial they opened in 1984 in Seattle. "We fill a variety of lodging needs for a diverse clientele with wide-ranging interests. Unlike travelers to other kinds of inns, our guests are not single-minded in their interests. Business guests mix freely with getaway couples and tourists visiting the many attractions Seattle has to offer."

One location with a magnetic pull for aspiring innkeepers is "away from it all"—the idyllic little spot out in the middle of nowhere (except the beautiful countryside). A similar one is the beautiful old house or mansion that begs to be turned into an inn. That is what happened to Owen and me with Boydville. I can therefore advise you of the problems with this approach.

People can sit still for only so long before they drive themselves (or you) nuts. Then they want to see something or do something—shop, visit an attraction, swim, whatever. If you're a farm in the country, will you have enough to keep them occupied? You do not want to be in the position of baby-sitting your guests. You want to be able to enjoy their company (and they yours) without overdoing it.

RULE 2: WRITE A BUSINESS PLAN

"The bed-and-breakfast business," says Murray Burns, innkeeper at the Eastlake Inn in Los Angeles, "needs the same sort of talents, the same sort of up-front analysis, the same sort of ongoing control systems that any viable, profit-making business needs."

Business plans need not be terribly elaborate, but the more detail you can put into them, the better. There are a number of books on writing business plans, so we won't go into great detail here. Get one of these books and take heed of their advice. There are, however, some aspects of inns that will require adjustments to the standard business plan and some details that you might not think of including.

You should first decide how formal you want your plan to be. You might be able to get by with something handwritten on the back of a napkin, but if you write a more formal plan, you will be treating innkeeping *as a business* from the beginning.

When Dennis and Cindy Marquis were negotiating to buy Maplewood Farm in Gardenville, Pennsylvania, they realized they would only have half of the down payment required and would have to look to friends and family for the rest. Says Dennis: "Based on our knowledge of having worked at an inn, and being computer-wise, we put together a seven-page business plan, complete with three-year revenue and cost projections. We tried to prove that the numbers worked and that, with our acquired innkeeper skills, we would be successful and thus able to pay back the bank plus the private investors."

From these observations we naturally get:

RULE 3: RESEARCH

There is no single resource book you can thumb through in the comfort of your home and your current job to answer all your questions. The burden is on you to investigate and compile data from primary sources (see the last chapter).

Do some background work on the area you're interested in. If you have found a mansion you want to convert to a B&B, what is there in the area to sustain it? If there's a town you want to move to, does it have at least one of the previously mentioned magnets going for it? And even more important, is the magnet known to the traveling public?

Even if there is an attraction like a factory outlet near you, will it attract the kind of guest you want? We thought that Boydville's location two blocks from the Blue Ridge factory outlet center would guarantee us traffic. We put hundreds of brochures in the center, without stopping to think that discount shoppers have no interest in a high-end luxury inn. Shopping was, and remains, simply a neat thing to do for guests who are already coming for some other reason.

Apply common sense to your research. Use the resources of your local Chamber of Commerce, which in the end will be a good contact for you. (A lot of guests write local chambers for lists of inns on their travel routes. If you don't belong, you can bet you won't get mentioned.) All chambers have good research on the potential of their areas. They'll also tell you what other inns operate in the area, so you can estimate whether there is room for another.

Many states and regions also have publicly funded visitors councils or tourist promotion agencies. These groups have the same capabilities as a Chamber of Commerce but focus only on tourism. They may even operate a tourist information center; if so, you should certainly visit it. When you've opened your inn, you will find that you become a visitors center yourself, so you should look at what resources the operating ones offer.

Talk to the inn association if there is one. Most regions with any concentration of inns will have a local or regional associa-tion, and they will give you good advice, possibly even telling you whether an inn in their area is for sale. If the association president tells you there's no more room, take it as the truth. Or at least realize that you will have to come up with some kind of niche that isn't being filled by any other inn.

Visit other inns. Best, stay in them, and pay the full rate (*never* ask for a discount when you do this kind of research). Always tell the innkeeper that you are thinking of opening an inn in the area. Be honest about your intentions and do not take too much of your host's time asking questions. The good will of other innkeepers will be critical to your success; do not do anything to jeopardize that good will. When you say what you are doing, the other innkeeper may turn his or her back on you, but our experience has been that this is rare.

You should also talk to local bankers involved in the hospitality industry. Introduce yourself as a future small business owner who may well seek financing from that bank. Interview the banker. Ask about his expertise in the lodging field in general and inns in particular. Bankers may be conservative, but they have a wealth of financial data on business operations and the history of successes and failures in your area.

The Yellow Pages of the local phone book is also an invaluable resource. When the time comes to assemble your team (architect, builder, attorney, and so on), it will come in handy. The phone book can also help you answer other questions during your research, such as, "Is there a good Chinese restaurant near my new inn?"

RULE 4: KNOW WHAT YOU ARE

Inns are the ultimate in niche marketing. Every kind of inn that could be created probably has a market somewhere. You need to make sure, however, that your niche is not so small that you can't survive on it. Finding those guests that want your kind of inn requires that you be able to define clearly what you are.

Spend considerable time—you'll do it for the pleasure anyway—writing down what sort of stage you're trying to set and what kind of experience you're trying to create. Although we often pride ourselves on the distinctiveness of our inns, the truth is that at least some people perceive a kind of sameness in them. Really, does *every* inn have to put a piece of chocolate on the pillow? It has become such a cliché that even the Sheraton does it now.

Some writers have taken to mocking the worst aspects of the "typical" inn. Cynthia Gorney, writing for the *Washington Post*, heaped scorn on the stereotype as long ago as 1987. "What we have here are seventeen-room Victorians furnished in the kind of chairs that history museums rope off with little gold braids. We have hand-polished silver brush and comb sets here, and sherry decanters made out of cut crystal, and leather-bound copies of *David Copperfield* for your reading pleasure. I ask you. You want to read *David Copperfield* on your vacation? You want to sign over your weekly paycheck so you can tiptoe around a bedroom full of spindly things that look like they're going to smash to smithereens if you're the type who can't see too well in the morning?"

Heed this. Avoid the stereotype. In order to be a success, you have to be idiosyncratic, maybe even eccentric. You have to be, above all, more than people expect. If at least one guest a week doesn't say that, or something like it, you're not sufficiently different.

Carl says, "Innkeeping is a profession of chiefs, not Indians." Is he ever right.

The inn is an extension of your personality. Memorable innkeepers are people of strong personality and conviction. Their inns are not for everyone, which means that there are going to be people who don't like it. But if you get rid of your personality, you might as well be a Marriott franchisee.

RULE 5: DO A TRIAL RUN

Maureen Magee, of Rabbit Hill, made the most elaborate effort I know of. For two years, she and John ran a B&B homestay in their house. "We had two rooms in our own house. We lost all kinds of money because we converted the rooms, plus we were giving away dinners. We had predicted the losses. The object was to test what we had already said we were going to do." Maureen says it was "the most important part of our ultimate success."

Dennis and Cynthia Marquis of Maplewood Farm also tested the waters before diving in. Cindy says, "We learned what to do, as well as what not to do, while working as resident innkeepers at the Wedgwood for over a year. We opened our own place and hit the ground running."

As we said before, working as an innkeeper for someone else, either through an apprenticeship program, as an inn-sitter, or as a resident innkeeper, will help prepare you for the realities of innkeeping better than anything else.

At the very least, be an observant guest at a number of inns. Certainly you'll copy details of one or another, but you'll never duplicate a great inn.

4

The Financial Facts of Life

"THE BIGGEST MISTAKE THAT INNKEEPERS MAKE IS NOT
REALIZING HOW MUCH MONEY IT TAKES."
—Jean Hendrick

Most of us think that if you start your own inn from scratch, in
just the building you want, with your own brochure and signage,
and with preconceptions from a previous owner, you have a
better chance for your inn to be perfect.

Sometimes this is true—if you're the first inn there. But you
have to face one major fact if you do this: It will take time—lots
of time—for you to become established. You could be lucky and
strike a public relations gold mine (a full feature in color in four
major travel magazines), but you would be foolish to count on
it. And if you don't get lucky, it will take you at least four or five
years to get established.

On the other hand, if you buy an established inn, you will
have to pay extra for the going business and its goodwill, and
you may not know all the problems dogging the business when
you take it over (a chef about to quit, a housekeeper who drinks,
a slate roof that needs replacing).

Nothing is sadder than watching nice people who put everything they have into an inn get slowly ground down by the
harsh financial realities of inn ownership. I know of two inns

that opened in the go-go years of the late 1980s with commercial loans at twice the going interest rate. The owners cheerfully assumed there would be all kinds of business because of the hot market at the time. Guests were not particularly price sensitive, and they were in a mood to take holidays. The owners thought their inns would be full from the start. They were wrong.

How do you get through those first few very tough years? Often one partner holds a job outside the inn. This becomes the base that keeps the whole operation from sinking. Innkeeping is a tax shelter for this steady income. When you hit black ink and retire from the nine-to-five job, that's the icing on the cake.

You should have a team when you tackle this project. Your team may include:

CPA and lawyer. Find those with commercial and lodging expertise, so that you and they do not reinvent the wheel. They will review the books, suggest the best form of ownership, and write a partnership agreement.

Architect, builder, or contractor. You will need someone knowledgeable in historic renovations or, if your inn is starting from scratch, in additions and alterations. At the least you will need someone to make an evaluation of an existing building.

An inn consultant. He or she writes the business plan, with income and expense projections and the key assumptions behind them, such as occupancy rates and room charges. A good inn consultant is a kind of scout who works for you in unfamiliar territory.

A real estate agent. You want someone knowledgeable in commercial real estate, not just a part-timer in home sales.

You are the quarterback of this team; you must communicate what you are trying to achieve, or the team will not get you where you want to go.

In any case, it will take you some time to get established. I think this fact of life should determine what you do. If you have the financial wherewithal to hold out for a long while, then starting from scratch may well be the thing for you. If you don't, then buying (or leasing) an established inn might be very wise. Of course, there's no guarantee that an established inn will support itself over the long haul, either. Financial management is always important, even with a strong business.

Margaret Perry bought the Thomas Shepherd Inn in Shepherdstown, West Virginia, in 1989. The Thomas Shepherd had been in business quite successfully for five years, had a strong following and a good reputation, was in a college town and a recreational area, and was near national historic parks. But Margaret has had to work very hard to make ends meet. The major reasons: a new, and higher, level of debt service and a reluctance on the new innkeeper's part to raise rates.

As important as where your inn will be is how large it will be. On that decision will hinge all kinds of financial decisions: how much money you'll need to run it, how much repairs will cost, how much to charge, how much help you will need, and so on.

Unfortunately, there is no simple answer to this question.

"How much house can you afford?" is a charming real estate phrase that just doesn't apply in this situation. You don't really know how much you can afford without figuring your costs per room and potential income per room. One good hedge is to consider how expandable the property is. Is there enough land to add on? Can you do it appropriately for the style of the house? Are there other buildings nearby that offer expansion possibilities? Will there be zoning problems if you want to expand?

There are other considerations besides size. Will you go for all private baths? For other amenities like fireplaces or suites? The questions of how upscale you want to be is not as easily answered in the parsimonious 1990s as it would have been in the 1980s.

There's no easy way to tell exactly what costs per room will be. That would make it too easy. And if this sounds like a catch-22, you're beginning to get a sense of the difficulties.

THE FINANCIAL NITTY-GRITTY

Here is where you get out your pencil and tackle some of the worksheets we have included below. You will have to do this for every property you want to consider seriously. It may take years to find the right one, so start looking and practicing early.

The worksheet sections can be put together differently depending on the situation. We'll just list here all those items you *might* include.

One section is going to be your *basic cost of the assets* (amount you will pay for such things as the property, furnishings, goodwill, logo design, and closing costs.) This is essentially the final sale price. For starters, use the asking price for your figures, though you probably will negotiate a lower one. Into this section will also go your planned improvements. Break these down as carefully as possible. You need to get good renovation estimates from the area you are going to and then allow some extra. Everybody says it, and it's true: we all think it's going to cost less and take less time than it really does.

You need a section for *acquisition costs.* These cover your travel, research, legal costs, telephone, inspection, appraisal, and so on. An inspection by a contractor is a very good idea, since he can turn up a number of weaknesses that you would not see by yourself. Do not take the owner's word for this. Most may be honest, but people have different ways of doing and looking at things. What may be at best a minor nuisance to me might be a major problem to you. Identifying these weaknesses will help you bargain over the price.

When you are looking to buy property, keep in mind that there are limits to what you can ask from a current owner in the way of inspections before a contract is signed. At some point, he or she is going to get irritated by the constant coming and going, and you'll have to show that you are serious. You can include on the written sales agreement that these inspections can be made and that the results must be satisfactory. The usual inspection areas include water, septic, insect damage, environmental, structural and mechanical.

Even with the results of these inspections in hand, your worksheets are truly going to be estimates. Everyone will advise you to estimate high, since even in the best of situations you will miss something. As Jean Hendrick of Pilgrim's Inn on Deer Isle, Maine, says, "In this two-hundred-year-old building, there are things breaking as we speak!"

Another section is the famous *working capital,* that chunk of money equal to three months of operating expenses that smoothes out the times when your anticipated cash flow turns into a trickle.

You will then need to figure *operating costs:* utilities, advertising, insurance, supplies, food, ongoing repairs, outside services, telephone, amenities, replacement of linens, and so on. Calculate these in one-month intervals and recognize that they won't be constant from month to month. If you're going to be open only seven months a year, then some costs will be negligible for part of the year. Again, estimate high.

Now you need to calculate projected *income.* These figures should also be in one-month intervals, with attention paid to the seasons. Most inns have high and low seasons (connected by "shoulder" seasons) and weekly cycles within each month. Identifying the patterns will help you allocate resources for those times when you will need extra. Putting operating costs together with projected income will tell you when your *greatest exposure* will be, that is, when you will have the most cash dipped out of your money well. That tells you how much you have to have as a reserve.

A word about room income: It is a perishable commodity— much more perishable than a piece of fruit. If a room is not sold tonight, it must be thrown out. The room can't be blended as a smoothie or frozen to be made into banana bread.

In the lodging business rooms have a substantial gross profit margin. However, the inn's fixed costs are high (debt service, insurance, real estate taxes). Much like a hospital, an inn is expensive to operate whether or not the bed is occupied.

And the good news: the actual cost of selling a room is quite low, often 10 to 20 percent of income. The marginal additional cost of filling that empty room at your inn includes laundry, chamberperson, amenities, supplies, and a minimum utility cost.

Consider this example: you have a ten-room inn with an average rate of $100 per room. Your average expenses are $7,000 per month and your average monthly income is $7,000. You have 300 potential room-days in a 30-day month, so your occupancy rate is 23 percent. What is the additional cost to book your 71st room? Your expenses are fixed at a little over $20 per room, whether it is rented or not. You can see then that renting a suite at $150, a room with a private bath at $100, or a shared-bath at $60 will all cost you the same. But the income from the most expensive room is far greater than that from the least expensive. You work no harder, and your fixed costs remain the same.

This may seem a bit obvious, but it allows you to see the major conclusion, to which we will return in a later chapter: higher occupancy rates yield an increasing return, and more rooms to rent may give you higher income with lower room rates, or, in a good market, a better chance of succeeding.

HOW BIG?

As you do this, you realize that there is no easy answer to the size question as it relates to profitability. If you have four rooms, you own the house free and clear, and your occupancy rate is 30 percent on an average room rate of $75, you will have a very nice profit margin indeed.

I doubt most potential innkeepers are in such a comfortable position. If you are really starting from scratch, you may well have a large mortgage. Then the same occupancy and room rates may see you slowly sliding toward bankruptcy. You can quickly see that, with a hefty mortgage, the top amount you could realize is limited, even at an unlikely, and probably undesirable, 100 percent occupancy.

I know of one inn, Cliffside Inn in Newport, Rhode Island, that manages over 95 percent occupancy in season with an average room rate of well over $100, but it has been in business for ten years, and its new owners have put considerable money into marketing and improvements. Cliffside has 11 rooms and is a true bed-and-breakfast inn. It was purchased from the original owner in 1988; it had a high occupancy because the area is extremely popular with tourists, and the occupancy rate has gone up since.

New innkeepers overestimate their potential income. The standard occupancy rate is 30 to 50 percent. This may be disappointing to you; aspiring innkeepers typically assume they will be renting at a minimum of 50 percent when they start out. But the case of Cliffside shows that if you are careful in the property you purchase, you can do very well indeed.

Our discussions with innkeepers have turned up a strong sense of what size is required to be profitable. It is hard to make money on an inn of fewer than eight rooms if you have any substantial property or mortgage and if your occupancy rate is less than 40 percent. A smaller inn must be taken on with great care. You'll need to spend more time than you think making sure that you will have a good location with high occupancy potential, and you'll need to leave yourself plenty of working capital.

Carl found that the original six-room Wedgwood wasn't big enough to satisfy the demand that it had in large part created itself; now he and Dinie have 18 rooms in three separate inns. Although there are now more headaches in the operation, at least there is more cash flow to work with. One other major advantage, Carl says, is that "it actually became easier to run as we got larger, because we were able to hire staff."

Heinz Haibach of the Millstone Inn says that his 11 rooms are four short of what he would like to have for genuine profitability.

The problem with growing is that you can lose touch with the personality of the true B&B. This may be the hardest part of innkeeping: getting the size (and price) right so that you can keep the property up, have a reasonable life, and yet keep the personality that brought you into innkeeping in the first place.

My opinion is that you are most successful when you have a homestay of three rooms or fewer or an inn of ten rooms or more. The range from four to nine rooms seems to be the hardest to make profitable. Over 20 and you are into the hotel business.

Maureen Magee says that she has learned that 18 rooms is the maximum she can manage and still maintain the personal contact with guests that makes Rabbit Hill so special. I suspect that she knows better than almost anyone; she and John have 21 rooms in the inn, and they are very energetic people who pay painstaking attention to detail. If they say the inn loses its personal touch at 19, then very few people would be able to manage more. Some probably do, but they have to be exceptional.

Gretchen Carroll, owner of Hillbrook Inn in Summit Point, West Virginia, ran her inn first at four rooms, then at five, for almost seven years. Even with a fine restaurant, high prices, a good occupancy rate on weekends, and a gross as high as $350,000, she had to struggle. Now she is undertaking an expansion to 15 rooms, which will allow her to hire more help, host conferences, and use her grounds for larger catered events. And she does expect that to change the character of her place.

HOW MUCH INCOME?

You now have two ways to calculate the value of your enterprise. One is your *equity,* which is the price you paid, improvements you make, and increasing value of your real estate. This is not liquid and is only useful to you while you have your business as security for a loan, if you need one. In some cases, you may be able to sell stock to get more working capital, but most inns do not.

Your *gross profit* is what you get after expenses and before taxes and depreciation. Your profit is what enables you to operate. If you ever have to dip into equity for operating income, you should be nervous. The exception, of course, is your working capital, which you have purposefully set aside to get you through the early years and times of slow cash flow.

For a working inn, equity is irrelevant to your operations. Gross profit and cash flow are what count.

After you figure your tax deduction—including depreciation (let your accountant figure this), you get pre-tax profit. Then, after you pay those income taxes, whatever is left over is net. Given the way inns work, any positive net profit is good (some people say this is true of any business) and even negative net profit isn't all bad. (As long as it doesn't go on too long or get too high, it can shelter the salary you pay yourself). You have to accept that you aren't going to make lots of money in this business, but you can have a good life on a very small income because so many of your expenses as owner and manager can be covered by the inn. As Kit Riley, a Denver real estate agent, consultant, and former innkeeper says, "The profit in inn ownership really comes when you sell it."

BUYING AN ESTABLISHED BUSINESS

If you buy an established inn, much of the work has been done for you. You pay more for it, but you should get quite a bit in return.

Before you rule out starting from scratch, however, remember that there are some considerable difficulties in evaluating a going proposition. Here are some questions you should be prepared to find answers to (and not necessarily by asking current owners or real estate agents):

• What is the annual percentage of occupancy? Is it high enough for the area? If not, why?

• Will you be able to retain current guests? Do you even want to?

• Is the property up to code and current in its licensing? If not, will this be difficult to achieve?

• Will you have room for expansion if you want to? Will local zoning permit you to expand?

• What are any and all zoning restrictions on the property?

• Does the business owe any back taxes? The last thing you want is a huge tax liability you hadn't planned for. One of the worst faults of poor innkeepers is that they don't pay the state. The state does not forgive.

• Does the owner insist that more is taken in than shows on the books? This surprisingly common assertion, besides being dishonest and illegal, makes an accurate income projection impossible. If you find yourself taking such an assertion seriously, you are letting your desire for a particular property overtake your good sense. You cannot trust any statement from someone who makes that assertion. Back off and get out.

- Is there evidence of deferred maintenance?
- Is the business involved in any legal actions such as liability suits or claims for nonpayment?

You and your accountant will need to see the financial records eventually. If you are a serious buyer and have been properly qualified by your agent, this shouldn't be a problem. Look at three years' worth of records. The books you will see probably haven't been audited, and you may not be able to evaluate them. This is when you should ask for help from your accountant; he or she will ask questions about the figures that may not occur to you. Beware of any handwritten books that look like they were all done at once (I have seen this). Usually they *were* done at once and therefore bear no relationship to the business.

New rules governing bank lending make it unlikely that you are going to be fooled into paying more for a property than it is worth, but you still have to beware of a number of things, especially if you are putting up a lot of equity; banks are only obliged to protect the amount of their loan. So, as when you start from scratch, get a qualified building inspector to tell you where the flaws are. Get a reasonable estimate of the cost of repairs and improvements. All of this has to go into your worksheets.

An additional check on the honesty and accuracy of the financial records (inaccurate ones are not necessarily dishonest) is to compare sales tax records to income tax records. Of course, the only income tax returns may be the owner's personal ones, which he or she may not be willing to share.

Be very specific about what the sales price includes in the way of equipment and furnishings. You don't have to enumerate every sheet and bar of soap, of course, but some reasonable accounting of inventory, by room, must be made. Remember, whatever isn't there you are going to have to buy, and all those little things are expensive when you have to buy a bunch of them. It can easily cost $1,000 to appoint one bed attractively, and $500 for a bathroom. Enough of those charges and you'll find yourself over budget very quickly.

Allow for a transition and renovation period, and figure out what to do with the staff (if any). Unless you believe the business is being run in a slipshod way, you will probably do best to keep whatever employees currently work there, even if you change their duties.

GO FIGURE

For the sake of comparison, here is a set of figures for three different purchasing possibilities. Cozy Corners is a going inn with four rooms, and Prosperity Hill is a going inn with ten rooms. We assume the new owners move in and start operating the first day. For income, we assume 50 percent occupancy at an average room rate of $100 (which are industry averages for well-managed, upscale mature inn businesses). In subsequent years, we assume a 5 percent annual increase in occupancy and a 2 percent increase in rates. Scratch Inn is a potential six-room inn that needs renovation and has not been operating as an inn—a true from-scratch proposition. We assume no occupancy at all for the first year (renovations, after all, take time), and, because the business is new, an $80 room rate for two years, with occupancy percentages at 18 percent and 24 percent in those two years. (These are reasonable assumptions, based on experience. We aren't trying to be discouraging.)

If the figures in the accompanying table don't frighten you about starting from scratch, they should. They're accurate for the situations they describe (we've had experience with all three). And we're assuming that you've chosen a pretty good location. After four years, Scratch Inn will probably look better, but it will still be years more before it does as well as the others.

On the brighter side, the monthly payment in each of these cases will make some difference in net profit. Probably the monthly payment for Cozy Corners will be about $3,000, for Prosperity Hill about $4,000, and for Scratch Inn, about $1,500.

There are differences that don't show up in the comparisons. For example, you see basically all the expenses for Scratch Inn in its first year of operation, whereas the other two will have food, staff, and other expenses to figure in. Insurance is more expensive for the more successful inn, though the income stream should bear it easily. These details you can see only in your month-by-month worksheets. A going inn will have books,

with actual expenses, that you can examine. You'll have to estimate for a from-scratch proposition.

	(Cozy Corners) 4-Room Going inn	(Prosperity Hill) 10-room Going inn	(Scratch Inn) 6-room From scratch
Price	$395,000	$650,000	$200,000
Down payment	98,750	162,500	50,000
Closing costs	23,700	39,000	12,000
Inventory	3,500	6,000	10,000
Other costs			
Moving	7,000	7,000	7,000
Deposits	2,550	3,000	6,000
Rent, Living	0	0	18,000
Approval process	0	0	12,000
Renovations	6,000	8,000	150,000
Furnishings, fixtures, equipment	2,800	4,000	80,000
Cost of assets (out of pocket)	$144,300	$229,500	$345,000
Working capital	30,000	30,000	70,000
Total cash needs (first year)	$174,300	$259,500	$415,000
Revenue projection			
Year 1	$73,000	$182,500	0
Year 2	81,906	204,765	$31,536
Year 3	91,139	227,848	42,048

For the going concerns, you can see that buying the larger inn
is the better investment (assuming you can afford it). With a
cash stream averaging $15,000 a month, a $4,000 payment looks
a lot more reasonable than $3,000 on a cash stream of about
$6,000 a month.

The purchase cost per room of Cozy Corners ($98,750) is
much higher than for Prosperity Hill ($65,000), proving again
that it's better to buy in volume. The cost per room for Scratch
Inn is about $70,000, including renovations, putting its room

costs above Prosperity Hill as well. Costs will be greater to operate Prosperity Hill, but revenue will be much higher.

So the return on investment (ROI) will also favor the larger
inn. ROI is a ratio of net pre-tax profits to total tangible assets.
For example, Cozy Corners' assets are about $144,000. Its projected
pre-tax net profit is probably about $15,000 (with careful man-
agement). The ROI is therefore about ten percent.

Cozy Corners will always stay cozy and will show its greatest
return to its owners when it sells. Prosperity Hill will continue
to grow stronger over the years, as more money to reinvest in
marketing, renovations, and improvements becomes available.
Scratch Inn's long-term future is hard to project. We would have
to make more assumptions in order to do that, but it plainly will
never catch up to Prosperity Hill's profits, or to its ROI.

In all cases you come up against the plain fact that *economies
of scale* give you a greater return. Economies of scale come
when you are doing things on a large enough scale that the initial
fixed costs are spread over a larger base, thus lowering the cost
per unit and increasing the profit per unit. (These terms no
doubt seem a bit distasteful for the innkeeper who wants to create
a romantic retreat, but it's a lot easier to create romance when
you have the resources.)

Hard figures put together by the Professional Association of
Innkeepers International bear this out. According to its 1989
survey of the bed-and-breakfast business, the larger the size, the
greater the return. The report says: "Smaller (two- to four-room)
properties do not make money. With six to seven rooms, the
owner-innkeeper starts making a profit. An inn with eleven to
twenty rooms is averaging an 8.23 percent return on initial investment including owner time (excludes property appreciation).
With more than twenty rooms, owners see a 28.7 percent return."

We'll look more carefully at Scratch Inn in the next chapter.
After all, the decision about starting up doesn't depend entirely
on financial considerations, and only you know if it's the way
you want to go.

WRITING A BUSINESS PLAN

Writing a business plan for your inn will serve a lot of purposes.
Most people think a business plan is necessary only if you need
to raise money from investors or banks (and almost all of us
need loans from time to time). But even if you are relying on

your own resources, it helps to have an outline of what you thought you were going to do when you started, so you can check your progress. And if you have an active partner, as most of us do, it is a formal statement about how money gets spent, on what schedule, and what is expected from the expenditures.

You won't be able to complete your business plan until you have selected your property, but you can work at it from various angles as you narrow your search and come to know your resources.

As you work on your plan, you will discover that you do it in pieces and not from beginning to end. You'll work first on some numbers, such as how much you have to spend and what some of your fixed costs are. Then you'll find you can't fill in some of the numbers without some research. That research will lead you to a descriptive section of the plan, before bringing you back to the numbers.

A business plan form has become reasonably conventional. The basic parts of a plan and what should go in them are described below.

Executive summary

Every plan begins with a precis, or summary. You write it last, when you have a plan to summarize, and then you put it first. It describes your hopes and dreams and objectives in plain, direct language. Writing down your dreams sheds some light on them, so don't be surprised if this part causes a bit of pain.

Think of yourself as a banker when you write and read this part of your plan. If in a few pages you cannot convince the skeptic in you that your plan will work, it probably won't. One of the reasons to write it last is so that you won't be tempted to manipulate the numbers in your plan.

The executive summary has an introductory paragraph or two that should capture your excitement about your inn and explain what ambience you are trying to create.

Several paragraphs summarizing each section of the plan follow the introduction. Enough financial detail should be included in the summary to give a good sense of the viability of the project. Executive summaries are often written as expanded tables of contents; if that form suits you, then use it.

Description of purpose

In a brief section of a page or so, describe your proposed inn, where it will be, what clientele you want to serve, and what your business goals are.

Here is where you separate yourself from other inns in your area. What are you going to offer that distinguishes you from them? Or, if it makes sense because of the amount of business, how will being similar work to your advantage?

Show how your inn fills a need in the marketplace. Don't just rely on generalizations here; place your own inn in context.

Detailed description of inn

Put here all the detail you can about what sort of atmosphere you want to create, who you think your guests will be, and how you will cater to them. This is the section of your plan you will come back to see what will be appropriate in terms of design. If you can state your ideas clearly and then fill that out with convincing details, you will be able to carry others along with your vision. If you cannot, you've discovered a weak spot in your new enterprise.

This part will be useful for two partners, who may suddenly discover they have differing views. One may want to put candles all through the inn, whereas the other might think that is expensive, dangerous, and tiresome. Putting details on paper will show up these disagreements early and allow you to work them out, a preferable alternative to having an argument in the middle of the dust of renovation. These written details will also be helpful when you are creating your brochure.

You can work on these two sections before you look at much property. Keep in mind, though, that you may not find the perfect property to allow you to carry out these plans. If you plan to do a mountain aerie with rustic appointments catering to an outdoor crowd, you'll avoid certain kinds of buildings. But you may run into the perfect Victorian in a village at the foot of the mountains and fall in love with it. Then you'll have to rethink everything.

Our point is that creating your "perfect" inn is an organic process. It will evolve with experience and change over time. The non-negotiable points in your model will become clear, as well as the areas where there is room to give. Let your ideas evolve as you refine them.

Marketing Plan

Your marketing plan is essential, especially if you are starting from scratch. You cannot simply open an inn and expect that your market will walk up to you. It won't.

Let me rephrase. It *probably* won't. Heinz Haibach says he opened Millstone Inn by putting a sign out on the road. The first guests walked in. But he did advertise later on, and he was in an enormously popular tourist area served by only one east-west road. In season, there is no lack of guests in that part of North Carolina.

If you buy an established inn, your marketing plan will focus on increasing business, or reaching out to a new clientele.

Essentially, your plan should have two parts: market research and selling activities.

Market research and analysis proves to you and your potential investors that you do have a market.

Although travel is big business, only a small part of the traveling public goes to inns, and it divides further according to kind of inn. Budget-conscious travelers will go for homestays; affluent professionals, business owners, and executives are drawn by the upscale B&B or country inn. You need to know if the kind of people you want to appeal to will want to come to your inn.

So do some informal research among people like the ones you want to reach. Talk to travel editors, if they are willing, and to other innkeepers. Stand outside tourist information centers in your area and ask questions (dress nicely and carry a clipboard on which to take notes). Visit with travel professionals in your area; you'll find them at the Chamber of Commerce, regional tourist bureaus, and inn associations. If there are no resources or other hospitality properties in the area, be wary. You may be in the wrong place!

After you are convinced that you have a market, focus on your selling activities. This will include some advertising, but advertising in the traditional mode is usually not effective for the small or medium-sized inn. Putting an ad in the newspaper draws almost no business (such travelers are usually price conscious and shop down the column looking for the best bargain), magazines very little, and radio and television almost none. And these are very expensive outlets. A quarter-page full-color ad in a regional travel magazine can cost you as much as $3000 and get you only five guests. By the next month you're forgotten.

In Chapter 6 we discuss the methods that work to get your inn noticed. You will need to adapt those ideas for your inn and put in your business plan the ones you are going to use. Your marketing budget will be very limited for the job it has to do, so you must take great care to spend wisely.

Operations

Under this heading go the details of how you will get your inn going and keep it running. This should be the easiest part of your plan. It should address these issues:
- How you will undertake renovation and how long that will take
- When you plan to start marketing and with what expenditures
- How you will handle growth
- Where will you get labor, either full-time or contract
- How you will deal with licensing and zoning, if they haven't been done

What you are doing in this section is supporting your requirements for capital and proving that you have estimated accurately.

Inns—like all new or expanding businesses—often founder on this issue. *The single most common cause of new business failure is running out of money.*

Management plan and organization

Management issues are tied to how you are organized. The bigger the company and the more formal the organization, the more people you are going to need to operate it. A simple sole proprietorship makes you the owner and manager. A full-scale corporation will require officers and a board of directors.

Sole proprietorship. The sole proprietorship is the simplest form of organization. You own everything, it's all reported on your personal income tax return (with some additional forms, of course), and you get whatever profit (or loss) you make in your venture.

The disadvantage of the sole proprietorship is that you are liable for all losses. If you go bankrupt, your creditors can go after you for everything you have (within reason). If you have a liability suit and lose, then all your personal estate is game.

This is an issue of considerable importance for innkeepers, who usually have everything they own in their business. If you lose such a suit, you really do lose everything. So a sole proprietorship, though simple to operate, does expose you to more risk. Most American businesses have chosen this form.

Partnership. A partnership is more complicated than the sole proprietorship, but not much. You will want to draw up a partnership agreement, and take care of all the issues of who owns how much equity, how you bring the venture to an end should that be necessary, and how to handle the withdrawal or death of one of the partners.

In a partnership, as in a sole proprietorship, the partners have the full liability, with the same disadvantages as the sole proprietorship.

There are *limited partnerships,* in which the general partner bears most of the liability and is the active manager. Other partners are limited in liability. This form is often for prospective inn owners who need help in coming up with the down payment. Such limited partnerships can be unstable, because the general partner has to spend time demonstrating to limited partners that their money isn't being misused. Buying out limited partners early is a good idea.

Inns are almost always partnerships, though they often do not have that structure. If you choose this form, you should write a partnership agreement that spells out all the difficulties you can anticipate. Like a business plan, it can anticipate and eliminate by previous agreement most of the unpleasantness resulting from major breakdowns in communication. It can assure that the business will survive a disagreement or the death or disability of one of the partners.

Corporation. There are two types of corporations: the regular (C) corporation and the subchapter-S (S) corporation.

Incorporation is the most complex type of legal organization. It is good for large-scale operations with complicated products and a need to operate with stability over a long period. If a company is expected to have a long life, it will need to change owners (shareholders) relatively easily without affecting the business.

A corporation has to register with the state of its incorporation, make sure it has annual board meetings, keep a stock and record book, file regular reports, and pay extra taxes for the privilege of this form of organization. It also pays income taxes *before* distributing any dividends to stockholders (trying the tempers of those who see this as double taxation of dividends).

Because of these various complications, there are not very

many corporations compared with the other kinds of organization.

Why, you ask, would you choose this form? For innkeepers, the corporate form of organization would seem to be an unnecessary complication of life.

There are several reasons. First, if you sell the business, you have a ready estimate of its value: the stock price you have set, plus its physical assets. You can raise money quickly through the sale of stock should you wish to do so. Most importantly, the corporation itself, not the individual stockholder, is the legal entity that bears liability.

This is important because, if there is a lawsuit based on a liability claim, it is the corporation that is sued and the corporation's assets that are at risk. Your personal assets are not owned by the corporation and are thus not in danger in such a suit.

Fortunately, most inn-goers simply do not go in for this kind of suit. Nor are inns known to have the deep pockets that make such a suit worth pursuing. There have probably been cases, although we don't know of any.

There is one other good reason for corporate organization: It requires greater care in accounting and reporting. As a result, corporations generally are not audited by the IRS as often as other businesses.

Still, corporate organization would not be worth the trouble for innkeepers, except for this interesting category, the S-corporation.

In exchange for certain limitations, which are no problem for this business, S-corps are allowed the protections of the corporation and yet can still have direct pass-through of profits and losses to the stockholders without double taxation. Boydville and Wedgwood are both S-corporations, so you know what advice we're likely to give.

Limited Liability Company. There is a new form of organization known as the limited liability company (LLC). Some states have passed this form of organization; more have not, but many are considering it. It allows the liability protection of the corporation and the simpler registration, reporting, and taxation requirements of the partnership.

The LLC may be an ideal form of organization for the small inn. If it were available in our state, I would take advantage of it. I urge you to investigate to see if it is available to you.

Back to the management plan. In it, explain your choice of organization. Lay out the role each owner will take. Introduce key people who may not be owners but who will be important to the inn. For each person mentioned, include a brief résumé in the supporting material at the end of your business plan.

Financials

If you are out to raise money, this is the part of your plan that bankers or investors will eye the most carefully. Even if you are financing the whole business yourself or are writing a plan to guide future growth, write this for yourself. It will give you a way to gauge your expenditures as you start up your inn.

Do a summary projection for five years. It should be more detailed at the beginning and brief at the end (monthly for the first three years, then annually after that, for example). Use the projection to show at what point the inn will break even, when it will begin to show profit, and how much.

The care with which you've done the earlier part of the plan will show here. If you have been filling in the numbers for each step, you will now begin to see the results.

These numbers will be your guide. Once you start up (or are growing), refer to them often, comparing your actual performance to your plan. If there's a discrepancy, do something.

Your numbers should reflect reality. Try not to be too enthusiastic in your projections. We have suggested the return on investment you might expect for various sizes of inn. At the very least, you want to be operating in the black after five years; the IRS takes a dim view of operations that lose money over long periods of time.

Profit percentages are typically slim—it's a rare business that shows a margin of 25 percent—so projecting high amounts is unrealistic. If you expect a margin of 4 percent, in order to show a profit of $8,000 you would have to have sales of $200,000. Sobering, isn't it? Some of the expenses of running an inn will astonish you. The suggested chart of accounts from the Professional Association of Innkeepers International (PAII) has a separate line for towels and linens—not an expense line you are likely to find in most businesses. Says Dane Wells of the Queen Victoria Inn, "We estimate that to keep this building attractive to the marketplace and in good condition takes between

$20,000 and $40,000 of capital expenditures each year." Of that, $2,000 alone is for linens. Painting the building costs $15,000 to $20,000, so they do a quarter of the house every year.

Jean Hendrick of Pilgrim's Inn says the same. "Every year we just plow thousands and thousands of dollars into this place. We have restored and redone every inch at least once and now we're ready to do it all again. . . . The leachfield [septic system] cost $15,000. The new pump in Room 15 is $1,000. My tablecloths cost $800—I just replaced them. Redoing that wicker rocker— took $40 of wicker, just like that."

Include in this financial plan all the kinds of expenses and revenues you can imagine.

Your income should include:
Room sales
Restaurant meals
Sales of gifts and books
Receptions and meetings
Under expenses account for such things as:
Salaries (especially your own)
Benefits (such as health insurance and retirement plans)
Rent (if you lease your building from the corporation, for example)
Cost of food
Cost of goods sold (books and so on)
Furniture and fixtures
Accounting services
Outside services (subcontracted services like inn-sitting)
Auto expense
Advertising and printing
Legal fees
Licenses
Office costs
Remodeling
Maintenance
Utilities
Taxes
Supplies
Telephone
Insurance (liability, fire, and theft)
Dues, subscriptions, memberships
There is another category of expense that does not go into the

	J	F	M	A	M
INCOME					
Rooms					
Receptions & Services					
Retail sales					
TOTAL INCOME					
Office expense					
Equipment rental					
Furniture & fixtures					
Accounting					
Advertising					
Printing charges					
Auto expense					
Bank charges					
Commissions to travel agents					
Legal fees					
Licenses					
Maintenance					
Postage					
Rent					
Utilities					
Taxes					
Telephone					
Travel entertainment					
Cleaning supplies					
Insurance					
Dues, subscriptions					
Outside services					
Cost of goods					
Miscellaneous					
TOTAL EXPENSES					
GROSS PROFIT (pre-tax)					
(Income less expenses)					

J	J	A	S	O	N	D	TOTAL

monthly analysis: capital improvements. These expenses are significant, but they are not treated by the IRS in the same way as current expenses. They have to be spread over a period of several years (the number is always changing). For the purpose of working out your monthly analysis, you can ignore these. When it comes time to file your taxes, you will want your accountant to help you with capital improvement expenses and depreciation calculations.

Your best bet for performing this kind of analysis is a spreadsheet. I cannot pass by the suggestion that you look into using a computer, although Carl thinks they're an abomination and won't go near one. This is a matter of taste. If you hate the things, it won't be worth the anxiety and the time it takes to learn. For those of us who like them, however, they are a lifesaver for tasks from accounting and bookkeeping to keeping track of former guests and writing confirmation letters. (More on this in Chapter 7.)

The sample spreadsheet for one year should help you estimate your monthly income and expenses. Make copies for each year and enter the figures from your calculations.

Total the figures in the right-hand column. Then total the figures in the bottom row. The two sums should be equal. If they're not, you've messed up somewhere.

There is no uniform set of expense and income averages, although PAII is promoting a standard set of expense categories.

Your spreadsheets provide detail, but you also need a summary of the figures to make your plan complete. The earlier comparison of the three inns shows one kind of summary; there are other ways as well. However you arrange the figures, the summary has to contain all of the totals under general categories. The financial summaries will be the basis of most of your discussions with bankers and potential investors.

RAISING THE MONEY

Now, you have all this stuff written down, but you still don't have the money. How have all these other innkeepers—thousands of them—managed to do it? These are some of the ways; there may be others:

• Sell your home and put your equity into the inn. This is the most common method.

- Assets you or your partner have managed to accumulate, such as savings or investments, can be cashed in.
- One partner works outside the inn. The job income qualifies you to borrow from a credit union, life insurance, or a bank.
- Young professionals without substantial income or assets may require experience in order to attract investors. A stint as an inn-sitter or resident innkeeper will help.
- Attract investors in a limited partnership.
- Look into state economic development funds, which may provide low-interest guaranteed loans. Check with your state commerce department.

5

Putting Your Stamp on Your Inn

"LOOK TO WHAT YOU LOVE; LET YOUR INN BE A STAGE FOR WHO YOU ARE."

—Maureen Magee

Now comes the fun part: setting that stage. This is your chance to make your ideas and visions for your inn come alive. In your enthusiasm, however, be aware of the pitfalls that await you. Overspending and lapsing into clichés are two of the most common.

THE BUILDING AND ITS FURNISHINGS

Inns are, first of all, architecture in a location. Certain locations have certain kinds of architecture: Victorian at Cape May, New Jersey; colonial in Williamsburg; Spanish adobe in New Mexico, San Diego, and St. Augustine; colonial and federal in New England and the mid-Atlantic; ranch in Texas; farmhouse in Ohio; prairie-style in Illinois; log cabins in the Northwoods. But you find all kinds of architecture in nearly all places. The style of your house will in part be dictated by area, and that architectural style will restrict some of your choices.

Work within your budget. Don't try to create Versailles if you can't afford it. You always have to make choices about where you will spend your money. There is never enough money to do all you want.

What people first see is either your brochure or the inn itself. So your physical building has to have what Carl calls "curb appeal." (More about brochures in the next chapter). If you are a formal person (which is, by the way, not incompatible with friendliness), use traditional signage and formal gardens. If you love flowers, plant them everywhere. If you like the country theme, have a plow or old wagon as part of your sign. Some people might find this hokey, but you're not looking for them as your guests. You're looking for people who like what you like.

Don't overspend on the facade. Every innkeeper can tell you stories passed on by guests who were drawn by the outside of a place that looked fabulous, only to discover it was seedy inside. When we discuss marketing, we advise you not to falsely advertise in your brochure. The same is true for the outside of your inn: Don't promise more than you can deliver. Guests have told us of an inn out west, a brand new building that attempts to be a version of Tara (an odd thing for the desert, anyway). It has pillars that don't quite reach to the portico, and fan windows with dividers, but no glass! Anyone who knows the real thing can spot a fake at once and will never be a returning guest.

Seacrest Manor, an eight-room B&B, opened in Rockport, Maine, in 1973 by Leighton T. Saville and Dwight B. MacCormack, Jr., was named 1988 Inn of the Year by the readers of Pamela Lanier's guidebook. Leighton says much of their success is due to a philosophy of honesty: "Be honest in how you portray your inn, and deliver on your promises."

If you want to open a historic inn, you don't have to spend a lot of money for an authentic look. Be careful about putting too many priceless pieces out. Accidents do happen, and although theft is very rare in the inn business, you don't want to be the one who proves the exception. You also want to avoid creating an oppressive museum.

Most historic inns are either Victorian or red-brick colonial. It stands to reason, since those are the styles that were put up when the country was in its glory days. The colonial projects more formality than the Victorian, and so, to put people in the right mood, it requires a bit more effort on your part. Victorians have a lot of odd little nooks, which make decorating a delight.

In general, most inns make some attempt to be in an older building on the assumption that most guests want to "step back in time" (that awful cliché).

If you love these styles, by all means go for it. You'll have the advantage of familiarity; guests will have an idea of what to expect. At the same time, however, you need to realize that familiarity can be a problem. People can get tired of seeing the same old thing. Inn-goers are an odd collection of the loyal and the fickle, which is why it is so important for your style to be your own—something you love and are comfortable with, not something you copied.

When Victorian goes wrong, it tends to slide into the fussy and overly cute. I think some innkeepers go overboard with bed furnishings: too many pillows, too many coverlets, too many flounces, flourishes, furbelows and froufrou. But there are guests who simply love that.

There are kinds of inns that would be inappropriate as historic inns. If you are in an outdoor recreational area serving hikers, rafters, and skiers, you're going to want a sturdier style. You're also probably the kind of person who prefers that. If you want to serve families, then you certainly don't want fragile antiques around.

The rustic inn will always be popular, and there are many mountain inns that go back to the late-nineteenth and early-twentieth centuries. (Some of these can be downright primitive, but inn guests these days are not interested in the primitive.) In the Smoky Mountains, one of the top tourist destinations, there are a number of inns with different approaches to being rustic. The Esmeralda in Blowing Rock, North Carolina, feels like a lodge and was a haunt of Lew Wallace, who wrote *Ben Hur*. The Esmeralda had a period of faded glory, but has been revived and now has a fine restaurant. The same is true of a popular old lodge called the Fryemont Inn in Bryson City, North Carolina. One of my favorites is the Millstone Inn near Cashiers, North Carolina. It combines a spectacular view and a cabin-like feel with wonderfully placed fine furnishings. The atmosphere is rustic but sophisticated—a feeling that appeals strongly to modern travelers.

In 1990, Arna and Jeff Fay opened the Fox Creek Bed & Breakfast in Fox, Alaska, an old mining town about ten miles north of

Fairbanks. It's an Alaskan rustic inn, but Arna emphasizes that the inn has all the amenities, including two whirlpool baths. The inn is Arna's full-time job; Jeff is a freelance photographer. B&Bs are becoming very popular in Alaska, and Jeff and Arna believe they are selling their lifestyle and personalities as well as lodgings. Both were born and raised in Alaska, and they attempt to present the inn as authentic Alaskan.

These styles, historic and rustic, dominate because most inns are still in New England, the mid-Atlantic states, and California. As more parts of the country develop inns other styles will leaven the mix.

Then there's *eclectic,* a term often used to be complimentary about a mishmash of no particular distinction. But it can refer to a charming expression of an innkeeper's personality. Hillbrook Inn is such a place. Gretchen Carroll created a country inn from a Normandy farmhouse built, in turn, around a seventeenth-century log house. The whole thing spills down a beautiful hillside. Inside is a mix of pieces Gretchen has collected from all over the world. Turkish samovars and Russian paintings sit side by side with contemporary American pieces. Entirely distinctive and yet harmonious as a whole, Hillbrook is a perfect expression of its owner's taste. It enchants its visitors because it is so unlike anything else they would find.

There is a trend toward more informal surroundings. Scratch-ankle Farm in Beaver Creek, Maryland, is as odd and informal a place as you can imagine, full of animals inside and out, with broken-down furniture alongside some astonishing antiques. Host Coulter Huyler, now in his 80s, regales guests with stories and an informality that drives some away. Owen and I chose a much more formal style for Boydville, yet even our guests gravitate toward the more informal rooms and old-fashioned veranda. It seems that the world is getting interested in being comfortable more than in being in high style.

Given this trend, you will have to be careful to leaven the formality of your historic inn. Conversely, if you have an informal inn, exercise some care to show that you aren't just throwing your place together willy-nilly.

Jean Hendrick keeps Pilgrim's Inn rustic, certainly. But she's also quite sure of how she wants things done: "We are not going to make any compromises because we're informal. I'm not going to dress up in a long skirt with a little bow because that's not me. Whatever our backgrounds, good points, and faults are, the inn is also that." In other words, good, fresh food, comfortable rooms, cordial hosts, and no faded tablecloths will have guests coming back.

YOUR STYLE

You cannot be all things to all people. Your strength will come from your originality and your ability to fill your niche. Not everyone is going to like your place; not everyone has to. One of the major mistakes that new innkeepers make is to bend their presentations to what they think the caller wants. New innkeepers also fall into imitation. True originality can be scary. If it has never been done before and is not expected in your area, will it catch on? Can you survive until you find your proper guests?

Susan Schwemm, associate editor of *America's Wonderful Little Hotels and Inns,* says that, in her many travels looking at inns, she has noticed how certain regions have particular kinds of inns. "Inns all tend to be similar in certain regions," she says, "even to the point of serving the same kinds of breakfast." There is, it would seem, safety in numbers.

This is not an unreasonable assumption: guests in a certain area are more or less trained to expect certain things. New innkeepers will not go too far afield for fear of disappointing guests' assumptions. Still, you can meet many expectations and still make a virtue of difference. It seems to us that prospective innkeepers move into an area and get captured by the regional style before they develop confidence in their own. Most of us take quite a while before we're able to convey the real flavor of ourselves and our inns. You would do well to travel to different regions of the country to try out inns and ask questions. You should be stimulated in ways you don't expect and more encouraged about your own originality.

An area like Cape May proves the exception to our rule about striving for uniqueness. Cape May has built its reputation as a town of Victorians. Being different here probably wouldn't be a good idea. By joining together, the town and its inn owners have created an ambience for everyone. This has the effect of making your inn seem to be a branch of a larger enterprise. You may not like that; if not, don't go to an area that is identified strongly with a particular style.

The possibilities for developing your own niche are endless. A number of inns, for example, are Christian in orientation. This can work quite well if you make your focus clear. Bill and Helen Goodbrod run Ye Olde Library Bed & Breakfast in Jersey Shore, Pennsylvania, as a Christian B&B. As it happens, there is not much to do in their area, and the house is neither historically important nor filled with antiques. But because they've identified their strengths and played them up, it does well for them.

Bill and Lola Coons used their interest in nature to create Down to Earth Lifestyles B&B—as unusual an idea for an inn as you can imagine. Located near Kansas City, the house is "earth-integrated" and the approach carries through everything they do. In an age of increasing environmental awareness, a comfortable house with 86 acres and an indoor pool has to make people interested. Lola and Bill opened in 1982 and tell guests that they are "midwestern through and through, from our architecture to our style, decor, and food."

With natural foods gaining popularity, you might build part of your appeal around fresh ingredients from your own garden. Margaret Perry of the Thomas Shepherd Inn cooks with flowers she grows in her garden. Her guests come back often for the food.

Why style is important

Establishing your style is not just a matter of whim. It is essential to your ability to compete. You have to go beyond imitation of what is already out there if you want people to come to *your* inn.

When a veteran observer like Cynthia La Ferle says she's tired of the same old thing, you can bet this attitude will show up in her writing. And she is one of the industry's opinion-makers. If you can't get written about because you're perceived as just another imitation operation in a crowded market, then you lose the important advantage of editorial endorsement.

If, on the other hand, you can establish your own special ambience and style, you'll attract those writers, often quickly. Your object is to be one of a kind, no matter how many other inns are out there. Most likely you will create a new inn audience for your area by doing so, and if you increase (and satisfy) a new group of travelers (*and* all the people they will tell), you'll do some good for yourself and the other inn owners around you.

Bobbi Lane, publisher of a travel newsletter, *The Yellow Brick Road,* advises every inn owner to create a mission statement—a one-paragraph description of who you are and what you do. The paragraph could even be shortened to a single phrase, like a slogan, and used on all your marketing pieces. This exercise will not only help you focus on what makes your inn unique, it will also benefit your marketing efforts.

Maintaining your own style doesn't mean ignoring everything else. Keep up with what is going on after you open your inn. Innkeepers get notoriously out of touch as they spend more and more time in their own inns and see less of others. Standards change, and you need to accept these changes without giving up what makes your inn special.

BACK TO THE FINANCIALS

Once you have established how you want to do your inn, there is a ticklish financial issue left. You need to be able to project your income. If you have done your research with some care, you have some idea of occupancy rates for your area. With a good place for a sign, key distribution points for your brochure, and excellent relations with surrounding inns and hotels, you may be able to figure on getting 40 to 50 percent of the prevailing occupancy rate for your area when you open. You will almost certainly be disappointed by how low the actual figure is.

Be as conservative as you can in your calculations. As we pointed out earlier, it is not at all unusual for a new inn to have an occupancy rate of 10 percent its first year and build rather slowly from there. Although you should expect an increase of 10 percent a year at first, you might have more or less depending on how quickly your inn catches on and how low you are at the start.

Remember that your occupancy may well be seasonal. If you are in New England, you are likely to be closed for three to six months of the year; with a season only six months long you cannot have more than a 50 percent rate even if every room is filled every day you are open. If you are a weekend place, as many inns near large cities are, then you may have a rate of 28 percent—and count yourself lucky for that.

So unless you are absolutely sure and have plenty of evidence to back you up, don't figure your occupancy rate high. You need an accurate rate in order to establish your pricing structure. If you have no idea what your rate will be, figure 10 percent. If you have less than that, you won't really have much of a business anyway, and at least you'll know that you can support your investment.

Deciding what to charge

Pricing is one of the most ticklish questions in innkeeping, yet we have seldom seen it discussed. On your room rate depends all your chance of success; without income you have no business, and without adequate income, you lose your business.

Pricing is a delicate balancing act of what you want (or need) to charge and what the traffic will bear. If you set a rate that will give you a comfortable income from the beginning, you may be priced out of the market. You cannot charge $150 for a room in an average rustic inn where the rate of similar inns is $70. If area inns are so crowded that you could rent a hammock on your porch with no bathroom privileges, then you might get that rate for a time—or after everyone else is filled. But we wouldn't want to have to deal with your guests. And we wouldn't make a bet on repeat business by word of mouth. Some areas of the country—Oregon is one—have low rates in general. An inn that could charge $175 in Newport, Rhode Island, would get only $90 at best in Seaside, Oregon.

Let's state here one of the maxims of the hotel business: Every $1,000 spent building a room should translate into one dollar in the room rate. If we equated all the costs for Scratch Inn with room costs, we would get a rate of $41.50 per room. Of course, that would be quite cheap. Such rates would certainly compete with the economy hotels and motels.

One of the problems of pricing is the old notion that, because of the term *B&B* and its European associations, we're cheap alternatives to hotels. You'll hear innkeepers complain about this perception often.

Claudia Tzucanow of Brunswick Manor in Brunswick, Georgia, says, "We have noticed that many of our inquiries are from people who are hunting for bargains. They have the mistaken impression that B&Bs are cheap places to stay. When this is obvious, Harry politely suggests that they consider a motel."

It may be useful to keep a list of phone numbers of other kinds of lodging in your area, not just other inns. If you can get the caller to tell you what rate range they are interested in, you may be able to make suggestions. It's always a good idea for them to wonder, if you're that helpful and nice (a motel never is), whether they might be missing something with you.

Hotel chains have made what we consider a major mistake in the recession of the early 1990s: they have gone on an advertising binge to tell customers how cheap they are. Price is not an overwhelming consideration for many travelers, particularly business travelers who require service. According to one marketing consultant, "Such advertising tells the customer to pick hotels just on price. It destroys brand loyalty and turns hotels into a commodity."

Our business, even where we offer lower rates, must avoid becoming a commodity. We cannot afford—any of us—to advertise enough to survive as a commodity. And most inns don't want to compete that way. Customer loyalty is essential to us, and we can take a certain amount of wicked delight in watching hotels fall into the trap of competing on price, offering nothing to distinguish themselves from the competition.

A rich tradition of bargaining in other parts of the world has never gotten established in America (with the exception of car purchases), and pricing has always been a take-it-or-leave-it thing here. Although it's still not too widespread, we're beginning to get guests who bargain, especially business people looking for a place for meetings. Frankly, we dislike it; bargaining is most certainly not what we got into the inn business to do.

So to establish what the market will bear you have to look at other prices. Cast a large net—all lodging establishments within a ten-mile radius. If you have a more sparsely populated area, then widen your circle. You will soon find that there is a range for your area.

Sometimes the pricing constraints will make it impossible for you to operate your new inn successfully. This happens when either there are not enough guests to support a new inn or the other inns in the area are so long-established that their fixed costs are relatively low, and they can realize a reasonable profit at much lower room rates than you could ever charge. This is a difficult situation for a new inn, and it means you aren't likely to get established without being prepared to go a number of years carrying financial losses. You may not be in a position to do that.

The easy answer to establishing a price is the traditional business one: add together the total dollar amount of your annual expenses and your desired annual return on your investment, then divide that figure by the anticipated number of rooms rented.

For example, for Scratch Inn you might have annual expenses of about $45,000 after start-up (we're being conservative, and we're not including much of a salary for the innkeepers). Figure on a generous rate of return of $10,000 per year, for a total of $55,000. With an occupancy rate of 15 percent, or about 350 rooms booked, this formula would say you should charge an average of $157 per room. If you have different rates for different rooms, as inns usually do, you're looking at a range of rates from about $110 to $200.

The new inn suffers from a double whammy. It has higher acquisition costs and, consequently, mortgages, than other inns in the area. And at the same time, they've got an established clientele and a built-up business. That clientele expects a certain rate in the area; if that rate is $140 a night, you may well be able to get a high rate. If, however, the going rate is $85 a night (and this is more common), you're going to have a hard time persuading the cost-conscious traveler to give you a try.

So now what? You could reduce your costs and the rate of return you are willing to take, at least at first. Suppose you take no return (not uncommon) and you figure you'll close down in cold months to save on utilities and upkeep. You might be able to get the total down to $40,000 a year. That would give you an average of $115 per room, with a range of $85 to $150.

On the surface, that seems to be doable, and things might get better as your occupancy rate went up. Yes and no. You're still putting your lowest rate at the average for the area. So if price is the major consideration, your least expensive room will not be booked until everyone else is half full. Under these circumstances, you probably won't make your projected occupancy rate, and you'll end up further behind.

One thing to note here is that in many areas there is a psychological barrier at $100 for double occupancy. Many travelers will balk at that point because they simply do not think that a B&B, particularly one in a rural area, should cost that much. Many innkeepers who have prices above $100 end up referring a lot of guests to other inns that are "more affordable."

After the $100 benchmark some innkeepers go to per-person

rates. For example, $65 per person works out to $130 per room, double occupancy. That sounds better to the customer. The drawback, of course, is when you have a single traveler. Most inns drop the rate for a single traveler back from the double occupancy rate: $130 double would be $110 single, for example. That's a lot more than $65, which you would have to honor if you offer per-person rates. The way around this is "$65 per person, *double occupancy.*"

Inns priced in that higher range are often used as benchmarks by others in the area who, by pricing $5 to $10 below, pick up the traveler who does not think there will be any difference in quality for that difference in price. This is one way for a new inn to get started, *if* the lead inn in the area doesn't feel threatened and is willing to refer people on.

Pricing strategies don't just follow the numbers, though. They are often an outgrowth of the innkeeper's style just as any other aspect of the inn is. You have to be able to quote your rates, believe in them, and make them stick. If you don't believe that your inn merits the rate you're charging, you'll start reducing it before you even hear what the customer has to say. Then where will you be?

Jean Hendrick, despite her very high occupancy rate, excellent restaurant, and stellar reputation, deliberately sets the rates of Pilgrim's Inn below those of other inns on Deer Island. That policy ensures a high occupancy rate, assuming that there are guests to be had (and in her area, there are).

You might call that a predatory pricing policy, and in some cases, it works. But it isn't something a new inn can usually manage, especially as the inn market matures. Jean has been in business for ten years and does not have a huge mortgage. She and Dud have amortized a large part of their investment already and can easily afford to defend their turf by a lower price.

Charles Hillestad of the Queen Anne Inn in Denver sets prices by watching closely what the local luxury hotels are charging and then pricing at less.

Pricing experts will tell you that trying to compete on price indicates naïveté on the part of the owner who tries it. Established inns, if they wish to be competitive, can reset rates low enough to beat back your challenge. Competing on price also means you are not paying attention to what you should be doing—offering a unique experience. You must differentiate yourself from the others by some means other than price. If and when you are well-established and are perhaps threatened by newer inns (if our business ever gets so predatory), then you might want to start competing on price.

There is good news, however, from Gretchen Carroll of Hillbrook Inn, whose rates are quite high. "I was told by a friend of mine who had successfully started an inn that I should charge a much higher rate than anyone else in the area," Gretchen says. "She said that people would pay the rate and actually think if it was that expensive it had to be good!" Of course, Gretchen's place is good, and so people have a reason to think it is.

You are now into the interesting area of guest psychology. Pricing doesn't depend on where your rates are in relation to the competition. Your prices also tell people what you are and what they are to expect. If you are competing on price, then you have to give a greater value per dollar than your competitors. Jean Hendrick does that. If you are competing on the uniqueness of the experience you offer then you need to convince potential guests that your price is an expression of how valuable this unique experience is.

The only way to know whether your guests will buy this is to try it. Inns depend on word of mouth and on repeat business. Guests may not recommend you if the price is out of line with the perceived value, and they certainly won't return. The greatest misery for the new innkeeper is self-deception. You may believe your inn is unique and exceptional. You set prices accordingly, you advertise accordingly, and yet you have no repeat business. That tells you something, and you need to listen to what it's telling you.

In general, inn-goers have been *quality conscious* not *cost conscious.* But the market is expanding, and new guests in the 1990s are not like new guests in the 1980s. New guests now *do* pay attention to price.

The old conventional wisdom among innkeepers was that the most expensive rooms booked first. Later, the most expensive and least expensive booked first. Now the conventional wisdom is that people are looking for value rather than luxury. Price is not the only indicator for them; they might well take the middle-priced room first. You have to do something to indicate that the value is worth the price, whatever the price is. That occasionally requires you to do some real selling.

Then there are the inns that started with rates that were too low and had a hard time bringing them up to the right level. Mae McQuade of the Split-Pine Farmhouse in Pine Grove Mills, Pennsylvania, made that mistake, and also has found herself helping other B&Bs get bookings that they don't pay their fair share for. Listen to her experience: "I started with some of the rooms too much of a bargain, and now I feel guilty bringing prices into line with market values. I imagine old timers are thinking that the bargains have disappeared. I know a number of independent hosts who do no advertising at all; they depend on word of mouth and referrals during the high seasons. They do not have the overhead others have to bear, so they charge less. I am a generous person, but I am beginning to feel it is against my best interests to send my overflow to these B&Bs."

We tend to agree. Especially since Mae is not much above them (at this writing her rates were in the $50 to $80 range). She does a brochure, pays for advertising, and otherwise builds business for her region—all of which eats up any difference in price. Predatory behavior by homestays is encroaching on an inn that is priced fairly.

Many inns in highly seasonal areas customarily charge seasonally adjusted rates. Some Cape May inns have five rates within any given twelve-month period.

One last thing to consider is the need to change your rates from time to time. How often? Most innkeepers review rates annually and often change them annually. If you do change your rates, keep the numbers even. There's not much meaning in a rate of $97.55, even though that may be your old rate adjusted for inflation.

Leighton Saville of Seacrest Manor says you "must keep up with inflation, but be careful not to raise rates so high as to price out your repeat clientele." You might offer your repeat guests the old rate for a period, in order to give them something special (and encourage them to come back).

The best time to raise rates is just before the beginning of your busy season. Your customers are less likely to be sensitive to rate changes then. But plan ahead. One time, after a two-year period of not raising rates we decided to do so, but forgot to tell people reserving for the busy season. As a consequence, we had half the month of October at old rates, and we had to be very careful not to quote the wrong rate to the wrong people.

MARKETING PLAN

In Chapter 6 we will talk about the specifics for marketing your inn, but here we're going to get you thinking about marketing in general. The best way to ensure your new inn has a fighting chance is to make sure you know *ahead of time* how you're going to sell it to customers. The marketability of your inn is tied directly to its design and execution. Working up a marketing plan is a good way to focus on what you're really trying to do: sell an experience.

Why do you need a plan? Because without it, you are likely to use your limited resources wastefully. Remember, marketing is very expensive. It can take three to ten percent of your gross revenues (the newer the business, the higher the percentage). This can be a big bite out of your new inn's income.

Most innkeepers follow some version of Carl and Dinie's three-point approach to marketing the Wedgwood: 1) minimize paid advertisements (none of us has that much money to spend); 2) maximize guest referrals and repeat business; 3) maximize professional referrals and free publicity from the media.

The Wedgwood's marketing plan has worked wonderfully for them. Here is their basic outline. Carl calls it S.O.S. for *situation, objectives,* and *strategy.* It has worked for many new innkeepers.

1. Analyze your **S**ituation. Some of the things to look at here include:
history and goals of inn
available investment
occupancy and profit potential
external market segment and size
market trends

2. State your **O**bjectives. They might be one or two (but probably not all) of the following:
increasing occupancy, market, profit share, or return on investment
improving image and reputation

3. Set out your **S**trategy. Use whatever means are available:
package, price, promotion, publicity
personal selling and advertising copy
media outlets
financing

Try your first pass on the back of an envelope. Summarize in one sentence how you see your situation. Do the same with your objective. Then jot down a rough strategy.

Here's an example:

Situation: Scratch Inn has good weekend business, but the midweek occupancy is very low.

Objective: To increase occupancy on Monday, Tuesday, and Wednesday nights by 25% over the next twelve months.

Strategy: Develop a marketing plan to attract new clientele who have the flexibility to travel midweek. For example, you can attract the following people: dentists, hairdressers, retirees, and business travelers. Try to reach them by using the following methods: advertising in specialty media outlets, offering credit for referrals from professionals, developing a special midweek package, offering lower midweek rates, or creating a direct-mail sales piece.

Notice a few important details about this rough marketing plan. It is very specific about each step. There is a narrowly focused problem, a precise quantifiable goal, and specific steps to reach it.

Further analysis of your situation may show that you cannot afford both the direct-mail piece and the advertising at the same time. Put them in preferred order, using affordability and expected return as criteria.

In order to complete the plan, you'll need to know what the possibilities are. Are you just blowing smoke, or are there actually some reasons for dentists to come to your town in midweek? You need to do market research to find out.

Market research simply means getting information that will strengthen your decisions and give you a solid basis for your expectations. You can ignore the facts, but do so with your eyes open. For example, because of an emotional attachment, you might decide to locate your inn in an area ten hours from any major population area, where the occupancy rate is low, and where your rates will also be low. If you're set on doing this, you might as well know up front what problems you'll face.

Your objectives are the key. It is important to make these goals specific in order to pursue them efficiently and to coordinate them with the rest of your operations.

The following guidelines will help you set good objectives:
- Keep them quantified and clear.
- Make them measurable so you can gauge your progress.
- Have several objectives so that if you miss one, you may accomplish others.
- Specify time frames, such as by month or season, short-term (one to two years) or long-run (three to six years).
- Set them high enough to be challenging, yet low enough to be realistic.
- Make a simple list or chart of your four or five key objectives.
- Set all objectives with an eye on affordability.

DEALING WITH REGULATIONS AND ZONING

As you begin the process of opening your inn, you're going to have to deal with the laws governing your operation. In Chapter 1 we noted that inn owners have gained a reputation for skirting the law. One reason is that the laws get more complicated all the time and we're often too busy to pay attention. Two things can ease this situation: setting up in a town that has experience in permitting inns or buying an existing operation.

With an existing inn the permitting process should already be done. Many inns operate under zoning exceptions or special exemptions to certain regulations (historic buildings, for example, are often given alternatives to full compliance with fire and building codes). If you're buying an existing inn, you'll need to make sure that all those exceptions transfer. If they don't you'll have to arrange for renewal or compliance before you take over (or have some assurance that this can be handled quickly and reasonably).

The major permits you need are zoning, fire, and health. Of those, zoning comes first and is regulated by the smallest jurisdiction that applies to you (city, township, or county). A quick visit to the city hall or county courthouse will get you early answers and will begin your acquaintance with officials who may have frequent contact with you as your business gets going. They will also probably be able to point you in the direction of the other two permitting authorities.

Fire regulations are usually handled by the county fire marshal or a local representative of the state fire marshal, sometimes by the town's fire chief. In many cases, there are exceptions to the rules if you have a historic building, if it has fewer than four rooms, or if it is two stories or smaller.

State-passed health regulations are almost invariably administered by the county. Food preparation is the most carefully watched. Many states do not allow B&B establishments to serve full breakfasts. If you do not want to install a commercial kitchen just to serve breakfast but you are not satisfied with a simple continental offering, make sure that the state will allow it. Otherwise you may be faced with installing a commercial kitchen—an expensive proposition, especially in a historic house.

There may be some serious problems for new *and* existing inns as the federal government increases its regulations. New legislation in the areas of environment, health, and disability may cause hardship for some inns. Although there are exceptions in most of these laws for small businesses (under 25 employees in most cases), those exceptions may not last forever. And whereas with local laws there is a tendency to "grandfather" existing operations, federal law usually gives existing businesses only a certain amount of slack before requiring compliance.

The law that may affect us most is the Americans with Disabilities Act. This law does not provide exceptions for small businesses that open after 1993. Even established inns should consider what is going to be required of establishments with five rooms or more: a disabled parking space for every 25 spaces or fewer; elevators for three stories or more; ramp access for public areas where level changes more than one-half inch; five percent of rooms available for wheelchairs; five percent of rooms for visually or hearing impaired (this requires such things as braille signs and flashing lights instead of alarms for fire).

The law does offer some concessions. There are exceptions for historic buildings, if the alterations would change the character in a serious way. Regulators are constrained to be "reasonable" in applying the requirements to existing buildings, and regulation should not inflict "undue financial hardship" on the business. Alas, there is a wide area for disagreement here.

There will probably be no exceptions for new construction, although this rarely applies in our business.

6

Getting Your Inn Noticed: The Importance of Marketing

Marketing begins with a concept. In innkeeping, that concept arises when you recognize a prospective guest's wants and desires and begin to plan actions to satisfy them. Designing your inn was your first step in marketing.

All the great marketers will remind you of this. Bernard Baruch: "The secret to success in business is to find a need and fill it." Marshall Field: "Give the customers what they want."

Some people do no marketing and still get business, but not many. At the very least, marketing will let other innkeepers know that you are opening.

MARKETING INNKEEPING

Despite all you will hear or read, there is one major reason people choose an inn over a hotel or motel: atmosphere. And the determining factor of atmosphere is the innkeeper. Innkeeping is intensely personal, and an inn is the extension of the innkeeper's personality.

We've said this before and we'll say it again: The innkeeper makes the inn. If you offer every amenity imaginable, if your furnishings are priceless antiques, if you have staff available to cater to every guest's whim, if your views are stunning and your location without peer, and you are an absentee landlord, you will probably do well. But you will have set a magnificent stage without a play; an inn without innkeeper presence is only a shadow of what it could be.

Market inns with innkeeping. You're not selling soap.

People who go to inns, especially devoted returnees, say a major reason they return is the innkeeper and the individual attention the innkeeper gives them. Travel writer Bernice Chesler calls this "the *I* in innkeeping." They expect to be greeted by the innkeeper, and they expect to spend time with him or her or both.

Innkeeper presence is the key to a pleasant inn, and yet in some guidebooks it is often passed over with a simple, "Of course, the innkeepers are friendly." Newspapers, magazines, and even most guidebooks regularly report on the amenities and the furnishings and not the innkeeper (pieces on the charming eccentricity of the innkeeper aside). This is a disservice to the innkeeper and the business. It's as though cordiality and hospitality are so obviously a given that there is no need for mention.

It is, at least, an assumption that benefits inns. As a given, it's one we are happy to have out there. (Unfortunately, there are inn-keepers who are not cordial, and they cause marketing problems for the others.)

One good reason to market innkeeping with innkeeping is to help dispel the mistaken impression that inns are simply cheap alternatives to motels and hotels. If you're going to charge guests three times as much as the nearest economy motel, you had better provide them with an experience that justifies the price.

THE RANGE OF MARKETING OPTIONS

There are various avenues to explore as you search for ways to market your inn. *Public relations* is work you do to get free attention. This includes personal visits to area businesses, successful placements of stories in the media (particularly travel publications), speaking and teaching engagements, doing interviews as an innkeeping "expert," and so on. Some of these things come to you accidentally, but on the whole you do have to work for them.

Travel writers, particularly, do not do a lot of digging for new inns to write about. Most will tell you that they have more in hand than they can get to and that there's nothing that distinguishes yours from the rest. Often they won't answer your calls or letters at all. This is distressing.

Promotions sometimes cost money, sometimes they don't. Promotional ideas range from sponsoring local schools to donating free nights for auctions to *frequent-stayer* plans.

If you participate in auctions (and most of us do a few), for goodness' sake limit the gift certificate to nights during your off-season or slow part of the week. Most gift certificates are worded something like this: "Good for any Sunday through Thursday evening except during the month of October. Valid until _____. Not transferable." Innkeepers who do not create such certificates for donations to auctions always regret it.

Maureen Magee is among many innkeepers who no longer give free nights for auctions. "We choose a charity each year and donate our time and money to it. We tell those who want auction donations that this is our charitable donation. We keep the inn itself separate." When you open your business the door will seem about to cave in from the pressure of donation-seekers. They seem to think that giving away a room is nothing to you. Their attitude is, "You have it anyway, and it's no extra work." Little do they know.

The frequent-stayer promotion may be just the thing for an inn in its early stages. Allow guests to accumulate credits toward a free stay by returning or by recommending other guests who stay with you. You can even work it into the theme of your inn, as do Edd and Sally Guishard at Brookside Farm in Dulzura, California. Their guests fill up an "egg basket" to earn a free visit. How many stays are required for a free credit is up to you—at least five, probably. In any case you need to make up some kind of formal device, like a gift certificate, with limitations, so that your free nights aren't demanded in your high season.

Other promotions are nationally run, such as Uncle Ben's Rice ("Ten Best Country Inns of the Year"), or Nabisco (in cooperation with the Association of American Historic Inns). The Nabisco promotion was a "buy one, get one free" offer on the backs of cereal packages. Many inns did not participate, but those that did felt it would simply give them wider exposure to writers because it was an unusual promotion. That's exactly what it has done.

The Uncle Ben's promotion gains a lot of attention for the country inns that win (B&Bs obviously aren't eligible, since rice is not usually served at breakfast). At the same time, Uncle Ben's gets associated with the ambience of innkeeping. This kind of corporate piggybacking is useful to both sides. Another example of this is Maxwell House's promotion for its old-fashioned coffee brand. At some point corporate piggy-backing could become detrimental to inns, but we're a long way from that.

Promotional ideas are as varied as the inns that run them. There are mystery weekends, romantic weekends, historical promotions, inn Christmas tours, and on and on. Norm Strasma's *Inn Business Review* newsletter offers regular listings of these promotional ideas. (You should subscribe to this newsletter: *Inn Business Review,* published by Norman Strasma, $39 per year, 105 East Court Street, Kankakee, Illinois 60901. Each year Strasma publishes the *Inn Review Yellow Pages,* the most complete listing of resources for B&B owners you will find.)

Publicity, as it is loosely called, can cut two ways. If you are ready for media coverage, it's great. If you're not, it can be a disaster. If you get a magazine writer, a TV station, or a newspaper reporter to come to your inn, you cannot control what they say or write. You can't even seem to be trying. They know what's going on, you know what's going on, but neither of you can say it. You must have a story to tell, and it has to be a good one. Simply saying you are a new inn is not enough.

There are 250,000 media outlets in the country. They need stories every day, and you can be one. But you have to avoid the obvious. Here are some of the questions an editor asks before he or she assigns a story:

What have we said about _____ before? What have we left out? What expert can we call on? Is _____ in our geographic area? Have we run too much on _____ this year?

Your best bet is not to try to create a story for yourself, but to attach yourself to a story the media has to cover anyway. Every year, for example, the media have to do Christmas stories. Editors hate Christmas. If you'd had to deal with a terminal case of the cutes every year for 25 years, you'd hate Christmas too. You have an inn on the Delaware, and Washington crossed the Delaware on Christmas Eve 1776. So you create a colonial Christmas. Make up a special cider with a recipe that's appropriate, and take samples out to the river where George landed. Maybe you could get some local college kids on the rowing team or a professional reenactment group to dress up. You'll be there to greet George with your cookies. A TV outfit *will* cover that (they do a lot sillier stuff, you know). You get mentioned. You get better than mentioned.

You can also do serious stuff: good-neighbor fund-raising, expert commentary, and so on.

Don't just think about the obvious outlets: the big city newspaper or TV station. Think of trade publications, sections of the newspaper other than food and travel, and specialty outlets of all kinds. You have to use your imagination. All it really takes is time.

Paid marketing includes your brochure and printed materials, newspaper and magazine advertising, travel agent commissions, newsletters, Yellow Pages listings, advertising in regional publications of collateral interest (antique guides, craft and tour brochures), and guidebooks (yes, most of them are really paid advertising).

You are unlikely to be able to afford a major blitz at the outset. If you are taking up an established inn, you may not have to do much more than make some subtle changes of direction. At the very least, you'll have to put your name on the brochure, business cards, and so on.

(Jerry Arndt, the insurance agent, says that he can always tell which inns are for sale; The owners' names are omitted from the brochure so that the cost of the printed material can be included in the sale.)

In your first three years, your advertising expenses will be relatively low, mostly because you won't be able to afford too much. In those years cast a wide net and experiment with different outlets. In the next three years, your expenditures should go up substantially; you should be able to afford it, and you have identified where your dollars will do the most work. In later years, your expenditures will go down (though not as low as at the beginning) because you are doing maintenance advertising. Word of mouth and repeat business will be doing most of your work.

Some of these paid marketing devices will be effective for you; some will not. Innkeepers say that most of their business comes from word-of-mouth referrals, from guidebooks, and from brochure placement.

USING MARKETING DEVICES.
Brochures and other printed materials
The brochure is the most frequently used form of marketing for an inn. You give it to guests, display it at welcome centers, mail

it to potential guests who request it, and put it in front of travel writers. It deserves a lot of thought, and there's nothing wrong with imitating the best.

Your brochure says a great deal about you and your inn, or should. Alas, most do not. Most innkeepers are not professional writers and do not have experience in this area. They aren't always sure what to put in a brochure.

The conventional wisdom is that a brochure may not get you a lot of business, but it can lose you a lot. Your brochure has to carry the image you have so carefully thought out; if a guest thinks your brochure is too flimsy or too slick, then you haven't succeeded. Your market should dictate the style and appearance of your brochure.

Unfortunately, when it comes to brochures, many innkeepers try to save by doing without professional design and writing services. But look at it this way: You're a professional innkeeper, and there are lots of details you just can't pass on to someone else. Similarly, you have to be willing to let other professionals do what they do best.

Hiring professionals doesn't assure a first-rate piece, but it gives you a better chance to get something that will work right away. If you do entrust this important task to professionals, however, you should not simply walk away and wait for delivery of the finished product. You must work with the designer and copywriter to help them understand the feel you want to convey. If they aren't interested in working with you, find other professionals to work with. If you don't spend time at this stage, you will not convey your uniqueness to potential guests, and you will lose out to other inns that look the same on paper and are less expensive.

If nothing else, underline this: *Guidebook authors use your brochure to write descriptions.* And these authors are pretty shrewd at reading between your brochure's lines. Guidebooks are a major source of customers for you. By the time you find out your description doesn't work, it will be too late to make changes for the next edition; you'll be years behind in building your business.

So how do you do an effective brochure?

Sandra Soule, author of one of my favorite guidebooks, *America's Wonderful Little Hotels and Inns,* is an expert on this. She does seminars on brochure writing. There's not room here to repeat everything Sandy has to say, but I'm going to condense as much of it as I can because it's so good. If you decide to become an innkeeper, watch for PAII seminars that feature her.

You can't go wrong with the simple trifolded, 8½-by-11-inch colored card stock brochure, printed on both sides in black or colored ink. A second sheet, 8½ by 3½, with specific details on rates, check-in times, cancellation policies, and other specifics that may change is often inserted. This allows you to take advantage of the prices of a longer print run—say, 10,000 brochures—without being stuck with the same prices for several years.

The front of your brochure should have your inn logo and name at the top so that it will show in brochure racks. Include your address and phone number on the front as well.

One side of your brochure should be designed for self-mailing. The postage is the same as for an envelope, but this saves you envelopes and stuffing time. Some inns do not do this. Boydville has a color brochure, and we do not want it defaced in the mail. Copper Beech Inn in Ivoryton, Connecticut, has a wonderful invitation-sized brochure. It is perfect for a mature inn that seems to be inviting a friend to the country. But these variations from the standard are done for specific reasons.

Commission a professional drawing of your inn. Unless you're going to have your brochure printed on slick paper (known in the trade as coated stock) with professional photographs, don't use photography. You can use what is called a *high-contrast* print if the subject does not have a lot of gradations, but this gives you something that looks almost like a drawing.

When it comes to artwork, presentation, photographs, and writing, please heed Sandy's advice: Don't make yourself look better than you are. Nothing is worse than overselling, and far too many inns do it in their brochures.

Sandy recommends that you include the following information in your brochure:

• Who the owners are and what they're like.

• What kinds of guests will feel most comfortable in your establishment. You may not appeal to everyone, and that's OK. (If you don't accept pets, make sure that's clear.)

• An accurate description of the inn: its era, architecture, furnishings. Don't oversell. Don't use the word *antiques* if you don't have them. (Antiques are defined as desirable pieces over

100 years old. Between 50 and 100 years old is semi-antique. Less than that may be old, but it isn't antique.) Never, never use the term *antique-filled.*

• Special touches that emphasize comfort: reading lights, exceptional mattresses, modern baths, storage space, whatever.

• A sense of the menu. Don't use meaningless terms like *gourmet* or *full* breakfast. List some specialties.

• Any refreshments offered at other times: cookies by the fire, iced tea on the screened porch.

• Cancellation policies, discount rates, and dates of opening or closing.

• Your phone number and address. Put these in a prominent place (or even several places).

• Area attractions that will appeal to guests.

One point that Sandy is very concerned about is how brochures deal with the matter of children. She does not like brochures that use phrases like "Children over 16 welcome." She finds this hypocritical. "There are other ways to discourage children if you feel you must. Stress the adult environment of your inn. Limit occupancy in each guest room to two people, thereby forcing families to get a separate room for the kids. The Old Miner's Lodge in Park City, California, has the right idea; their brochure states, 'Children welcome, but young ones find us boring.'" (More on this important subject in Chapter 7.)

The writing quality in your brochure is important. You may try to write it yourself, but nonprofessionals usually fall back on clichés, copying things they like from other brochures. If you write your own brochure, you must find your own voice.

Stay away from empty adjectives and clichés: *antiques, attractive, charming, country, cozy, deluxe, gourmet, elegant.* My nominations for overused words and phrases: *nestled, antique-filled, romantic, quaint, step back in time, charm of yesterday and comforts of today,* and *quiet* (especially when it isn't). Some words that seem to be coming in—and shouldn't: *scrumptious, enchanting.* There is a dreadful style of writing I think of as "inn brochure style." Putting all this triteness together, I give you the Brochure from Hell, so saccharine and cute as to induce diabetes in any sensible reader.

> Step back in time at Scratch Inn, where a warm
> country welcome awaits you in our romantically re-

stored turn-of-the-century Art Deco home. Enjoy the grand Victorian stair, our quaint rooms, our elegant period furnishings, the inviting ambience of the fireplace in our charming parlor.

Guests may snuggle in front of a cozy fire in the antique-filled den, or in the summer they may enjoy a country gourmet breakfast on our charming screened porch.

Pamper yourself in elegant luxury in an antique-filled sleeping chamber. Enter this romantic place of timeless tranquility and complete relaxation. Enjoy its character and charm of more than 75 years. Find delight in its beautiful antiques, the privacy of your lodgings, and the excellent cuisine served in the intimate atmosphere of quiet elegance. The past gently echoes throughout an elegantly restored inn that also preserves the gracious service of a bygone era. Step into history. Each visitor receives a warm welcome back to a bygone era. The casually elegant ambience is reinforced by guest bedrooms tastefully decorated with antiques and appointed with luxurious fabric and linens.

This is no joke; most of these lines are lifted from brochures I've collected over the years. No inn could be all that this one professes to be, yet inn-goers believe these descriptions. They are looking for these things, and will see them—even if they're not there.

Thank goodness for the tolerant guests, who don't complain when they get less than they are led to expect. Still, there's going to come a point when some of our guests will start crying out that the emperor has no clothes.

Yet to us the worst thing about this drivel is that *it makes everybody sound the same.* And that's what we're trying to avoid. None of us can quite escape the clichés; we all include a few in our brochures. The best parts of many brochures are the paragraphs that give the history of the particular house (or its acquisition). But at least give the reader a real feel for your inn.

I shudder to think that some of these hackneyed phrases found their way into brochures printed under our name. Learn from the errors of others and try to be fresh. If you aren't secure in your writing, hire a professional. If you can't afford a professional, find a pretty good writer who will exchange services with you. In fact, it is hard for anyone to write about your place without visiting it, so you could kill two or three birds with one stone.

Finally, proofread your brochure several times, at every stage. Get some eagle-eyed friends to read it over for tone and for errors. Your printer won't do it. "Brochures that proclaim the innkeeper's attention to detail but have typos are sending a mixed message at best," says Sandra Soule. Typos are *hard* to detect, believe me (detecting them is one of my professional skills). But ridding your brochure of them is essential.

Newsletters

Many inns do newsletters, and with the dawn of desktop publishing putting them out is getting easier. Your guests, however, may not respond as much as you like. They see newsletters all the time; some of them are quite professional. If you put a newsletter together and send it out to your guests, you may be disappointed when you hear back from only a few.

People are bombarded by so much mail that they barely skim most of it. Ten years ago, a 3 percent response rate on a direct-mail piece was considered very good; now half that is considered excellent. Inn newsletters are more likely than junk mail to be read, but you're not going to get a huge response rate. And remember, many of your guests may well be getting newsletters from other inns.Sometimes the more professional the presentation, the less attention an inn newsletter will get. A copy of a hand-printed letter can be just as effective. A letter addressed "To our guests" will often touch the right note. In newsletters, you are writing to people who already know you, so it is especially important that your personality come through. If you are odd, the letter should be odd; if you are caring, that should come through. If you are brisk and businesslike, so should the letter be.

In fact, the term *newsletter* doesn't quite cover the kind of communication you can have with your guests. There may be almost no news in it. It is more a reminder to let your guests know you're there, and to help them recall the kind of atmosphere you have created.

Have someone else read your letter, and ask for an honest reaction. Is it really you? Or does it put people off? Maureen

Magee sends out newsletters and gets a wide range of responses, depending entirely on how the piece was written.

After their first year at Rabbit Hill, John and Maureen sent out a letter that brought the kind of response we would all like to have: thousands of dollars' worth of reservations. We're going to reproduce it, with some trepidation lest you copy it. This is so distinctly Rabbit Hill that none of us could take it over without hitting a false note.

> To our dear guests,
> We purchased Rabbit Hill 1 April 1987, with expectations of hard work and of joy greater than work. It was our expressed goal to serve you and to offer our home as yours. Today we are filled with emotion that began building upon learning that Rabbit Hill could be ours. It is our dream come true and, happily, the reality of 'keeping an inn' has turned out to be even greater than the dream.
> Thank you for what you have written to us. Upon closing for three weeks last November, the first thing we did was re-read all the room diaries. This was overwhelming affirmation. We were filled with love. Your faces, voices, your laughter and soft conversations flooded this silent and empty inn, even if only in memory. You came here to become engaged, celebrate love, your anniversary, honeymoon, birthday, book publication, to rest, play, rediscover each other, visit colleges, visit Vermont, on business and for reasons that are known only to you. Later so many of you wrote to us, sending pictures and more pieces of yourselves.
> Maureen's favorite memories: that John could fix the commercial washing machine with auto parts on a Sunday when no one else would repair it; the people who fell asleep on the second floor porch and remained there all night.
> John's favorite memories: smelling fresh baked rolls at 7 A.M.; seeing so many stars in the night sky over the lighted church steeple; soaking in the pure tranquility of the White Village in the late afternoon.
> Emerson said the ornament of a house is the friends

who frequent it. You have been more than guests and
this house is well ornamented. Thank you all. Please
join us again.

Very simple, and very effective for the kind of inn John and
Maureen have created. It was photocopied on letterhead, including
the signatures. In other words, nothing fancy.

At the other end you have elaborate newsletters like the one
from Dane Wells' Queen Victoria in Cape May. It is done in colored
ink on several pages and covers all kinds of planned events and re-
cent happenings. Guests seem to like to hear about new renovations and additions to the innkeeping family (including its pets)
and to be reminded of the atmosphere. It's also an opportunity to
make a special offer that distinguishes them as returning guests.

Since postage is expensive, as is printing if you have it professionally done, newsletters are not an inconsequential expense.
Pare your mailing lists down to those guests who you want to
encourage to remember you, not those who were difficult or
indifferent or those who are so far away that a return visit is
unlikely (we do not include South Africa or Japan in our mailings,
though perhaps we should).

Paid advertising

Innkeepers are at best skeptical about paid advertising. Most
inns cannot afford the frequency and coverage that effective advertising requires. Think of how many times you have to see a
soft drink commercial on TV before you can match the product
with the commercial.

In any case, mass advertising is just not going to work for inns or
the people they want to reach. Leave the full-page, full-color ads
to motel and hotel chains, who will beat you on price anyway.

Nevertheless, there is a place for advertising in your marketing plan.
Advertising gives you exposure.

People need to be reminded you're there. Inn-goers want to go
to inns. They are looking for them and will go to a great deal of
work to find the right one. But they need to know you're out
there. If they can't find you, they won't come.

Even guests who have been to your inn and enjoyed themselves
there need to be reminded. Depending on your location and the
attractiveness of your area, guests may return once a month,

once every six months, or only once a year. For those who come less often, you need to do something to reinforce the fact that you are still there and still offering the wonderful retreat they liked so much before.

This gives you some real advantages with the type of audience you want to reach. You don't have to have that much exposure to be found, at least by the style- and taste-setters. In fact, inn-goers are far more likely to find you than are travel writers, who are not generally very good at research.

But there may be a number of inns in your area or of your type. So paid advertising is an opportunity for you to attract a segment of the audience that is already interested in coming to an inn but just hasn't decided which one. You need to find the medium most used by inn travelers for your area—a magazine, a newspaper, or some specialty publication. Advertise there with some frequency, and you will come to the attention of the inn-goer you want to reach.

Most such ads are in the nature of classified ads. They are small, one-inch-deep descriptions of what you have to offer. Usually you can include a picture or a drawing for a reasonable rate. Such advertising is usually not beyond your budget.

As success grows, you may want to go up to what is called a "one-sixth"—a fraction of a page usually one column wide and about four inches deep. That will run you several hundred dollars in some publications and up to several thousand in others.

Inns can be rated by entities like AAA, Mobil, and AB&BA. These ratings are useful, not just because the entities are recognized and trusted, but also because for a fee you can use their logos in your own advertising. These "endorsements" confer an immense advantage. How do you get these groups to rate you? All you have to do is ask them to come. (AB&BA is an association. You have to pay a fee to join, but there are no barriers to entry unless you are unacceptable by their minimum standards.)

In general, you won't be spending more than five percent of your budget on paid advertising. If that won't get you more than one ad, look for a magazine that does some kind of annual "inn guide" that is easy to pull out and save and place your ad there. (In the east *Mid-Atlantic Country* is the most popular such magazine.) Inn-goers do save these, often for years, and so you will get a lot of exposure for your money.

Guidebooks

Inclusion in these is essential to success in this business. That is one reason start-ups are so difficult. It takes a long time to get placed in the guidebooks, even if you start trying before you open. Once you are in a few, the rest will find you.

The usual publishing schedule puts most guidebooks out in the spring. Authors' deadlines are early fall. That means your deadline is no later than August. There are some exceptions, but not many.

The guidebook authors will want to know about you, so as soon as you have your brochure and some pictures of your inn, write a letter to them. Tell them you are opening a new inn and ask to be included in their book. They will send you a form and a price list if they charge. (Many do, but some do not.)

Guidebooks are proliferating. We have heard there are as many as 70. "Application or processing fees" range from $25 to several thousand dollars (for a full-color regional publication); most are in the $50 to $100 range now. Sophisticated as they are, most inn-goers don't realize that most of the books are paid advertising, with copy generally provided by the innkeepers. Obviously, you could spend your entire advertising budget on these publications, and it wouldn't be a bad use of the money.

The reason is simple. When people buy a book, they keep it for a long time, and they use it. Inns get reservations from books that have been out for years—and guests are sometimes astonished to find that the rates have changed considerably over that time. Some innkeepers have had rates quoted to them that were lower than they ever charged, even at opening. Accuracy is not always fanatically observed in the paid books.

The guidebooks that seem to work best are those that are not paid advertising. Authors of books like *Inns of the Blue Ridge* and *America's Wonderful Little Hotels and Inns* write their own copy, visit the properties they write about, and in many cases include guest comments. That isn't to say you can't manipulate guest comments (alas, many innkeepers do), but at least the third party lends credibility.

I dislike soliciting guest comments for books on the grounds that, if the inns are any good, remarks ought to be spontaneous. Your guests come to you to relax, not to be put to work. Other innkeepers, however, think my attitude is silly.

Carl suggests that innkeepers who can't wait for good comments to accumulate in guest books should put blank copies of an inn guide's evaluation form on the desk for guests to complete. Guests seem to enjoy wearing the hat of inn critic; they also enjoy reading other guests' "color commentary." Putting the forms out splits the difference between solicitation and manipulation.

Travel agent commissions

Commissions are a minor expense, usually ten percent of the published rate. Unfortunately, travel agents are not fond of dealing in inns for obvious reasons. They can't rent large blocks of rooms, where the profit really is. By renting an inn room, travel agents are usually providing a service to a client from whom they expect other business.

Another drawback to working with travel agents results from the major strength of the small inn: It's just as hard for a travel agent to know about different inns as it is for a traveler. As agents learn about inns, they may be more willing to book them. We often have travel agents as visitors, and they send the occasional guest, so we always pay agent commissions of ten percent. As the inn business matures, there might be more business from this source.

One way of encouraging travel agent activity is to have a toll-free number. Most inns that have "800" numbers say it increases their reservations from travel agents enormously. It seems to be an indication of "bigness" that says you are professional.

THE FINER POINTS OF MARKETING
On the phone

Selling is not something most of us do naturally. But when it comes to dealing on the phone, good selling can turn a casual caller into a guest. Pay attention to how professional salespeople work the phones; they know little tricks that will work for you.

You have to think of every caller as a potential guest, even if they don't end up staying with you. It's awfully easy to lose your temper with a caller who asks what seem to you to be stupid questions (and on some days every question seems stupid). If a caller is insulting, you might indulge yourself in a frosty insult or two—but keep these to a minimum. The old sales law is true: A happy customer will tell one or two other people; an unhappy one will tell ten. You lose a lot of business in ways you don't know, and you may find it hard to shake a reputation for snobbishness or surliness as a result of a poor phone manner.

Some callers are easy. Their hobby is to check out every new inn in the area. They often tell other people, because they like to be known as trend-setters. These callers are reasonably sophisticated about inn-going and will ask the right questions. Sometimes they're obnoxious, but they are very worth your efforts to be polite.

Referring guests to other inns is a service you perform both for other innkeepers and for guests. If you're helpful, you may well get that guest another time. Even the bargain hunter we all dread may be a future guest if you handle the referral well. (More telephone tips in Chapter 8.)

Little Things Mean a Lot

Here is a collection of marketing ideas in no particular order, many of which you may find useful.

• Curb appeal brings walk-in business and many lookers who wind up making reservations for a future date. How you look from the road is very important. Carl and Dinie joke that a portion of maintenance and landscaping expenses belong in the advertising budget.

• Include a business card when you pay your bills.

• Make sure your brochures are available where people will be looking: regional tourist offices, chambers of commerce, antique shops, interstate welcome stations.

• Invite a politician to breakfast.

• Give away extra muffins or cookies as thank-yous to referral sources, colleagues, suppliers, and such.

• Swap mailing lists with a similar inn located elsewhere.

• Donate baked goods or meeting space (but generally not rooms) at your inn for worthy community events.

• Participate in programs such as house tours and co-op ads sponsored by trade associations.

• Write! Comment on trends, issues, stories, or anything else in the letters-to-the-editor section of newspapers or through other media outlets.

• Offer trade discounts to your colleagues. It's a good way to learn from others, and the innkeeper can promote your inn to his or her own guests.

- Carl drops off a checklist of inn services with suppliers. "It's a chance to say hello and to meet new staff people who are potential referral sources." He also includes some of the Wedgwood's home-baked goodies at the same time.

Learn to act big

It is useful for innkeepers to start to think about a future that is bound to change. Guests expect even small companies to act professionally. That does not mean losing your folksiness or individuality, but there's nothing to be gained in trying to do everything yourself.

Through associations or loose arrangements with other inns, you should start working toward group marketing such as joint advertising, brochures, and special events. Groups give the impression of stability, seriousness, and all those other good things that impress potential customers. (For more on this subject, see Chapter 10.)

Jerica Hill and the Cabbage Rose Inn in Flemington, New Jersey, are two five-room inns that have joined together to offer enough guest rooms to accommodate small meetings, something neither could do alone. They send out a professionally produced mailing piece with a combined letterhead that makes them look like a group.

Give some thought to working with a professional marketing firm at some point. If you don't have the ready cash, you may be able to trade for services.

Never overlook an opportunity

Marketing means seeing opportunities in circumstances where no one else would. There's no way to predict what or when these will be.

Crescent Dragonwagon, innkeeper at Dairy Hollow House in Eureka Springs, Arkansas, is a phrase magician, beginning with her own name, which she created in the 1960s. For the inn's restaurant, she invented the term "Nouveau Zarks" for the cuisine. How can you resist?

Pat O'Brien, whose Blue Spruce Inn in Soquel, California, has been open since 1990, recently went through an expansion. Pat tells about an opportunity that most of us would miss: "I learned quite by accident how far fresh-baked cookies, hot coffee, and a few encouraging words can go. . . . We had a great deal of reconstruction done on the house. It involved many different workers from a wide variety of professions. We also did business with many suppliers. With each new contact, whether it was the tile setter, fixture salesperson, or carpet installer, I personally engaged them in conversation. I told them about our project and praised the quality of their work or product. My original goal was to share our dream with them in the hopes of inspiring them to do their best work. What I didn't bargain for was that these craftspeople became ambassadors for our fledgling inn. They sent referrals to us, told their friends about us, and made reservations for themselves in favorite rooms they had worked on. It was a wonderful experience."

Anyone who can come through major remodeling like that is a born innkeeper. Considering the way Carl always talks about taking home-baked goodies to prospects, we should make the innkeepers' theme "Say it with cookies."

7

Policies and Procedures: Save Yourself a Lot of Grief

"AN ABSOLUTE RULE FOR INNKEEPERS IS TO SET POLICY AND STICK BY IT."

—Arna Fay

Your policies make it possible for you to offer the kind of service that gives your inn its special character. They aren't (or shouldn't be) arbitrary; they're for the guest's good as well as yours. Guests are happier if they know where they stand and are not left wondering what they may or may not do.

Keep in mind that your policies, as much as your amenities, help define your inn. There are no right or wrong policies—there are only your policies. They are an expression of your personality and so will vary.

In the following discussion, we use several terms that it may be useful to define here:

Minimum stay: A requirement (usually during the busiest season) that guests stay a minimum number of nights.

Comp: Complimentary—a free night given for publicity or for other reasons you deem important.

Seasons: High season is your busiest, off-season your slowest. These are joined by the "shoulder" season.

Guest: A paying customer often referred to as a houseguest, reservation, or overnight lodger. Not a patient, client, or fare. An individual guest you know rather than an anonymous room number at a large hotel.

Confirmed reservation: A reservation accompanied by advanced deposit or credit card number.

POLICIES AND PROCEDURES MANUAL

Your policy manual will be important for your inn-sitter or staff. In your absence you want them to run your inn just as you would, but they cannot if you haven't explained things clearly.

Like a child who asks a question of both parents and chooses the answer he likes better, a guest may do the same with you, your partner, and your staff. You do want everyone singing from the same choir book. That's why it's important to have house rules.

When we say *policy manual,* we don't mean an encyclopedic tome that is intimidating just to look at. A simple three-ring notebook with index tabs will do. It should contain all the policies and procedures that are in force in your inn, as well as your ways of handling the many small details. It might even have a section on restaurants, attractions, and other information about the area. Keep several copies, or one on the computer, and note changes, additions, and revisions in every copy as they occur.

Include miscellaneous housekeeping details, such as where you keep soaps, sheets, and cleaning supplies, and any peculiarities about any parts of the house. Many things that you learn as you go along become automatic. If you forget to pass that knowledge along to others, they have to invent the wheel all over again. In large organizations this is known as institutional memory, and companies regularly lose it, to their cost. Small as you are, communication problems and lapses can create exactly the same problems for which we blame large bureaucracies. At least they have the excuse of bigness.

COMMUNICATING POLICIES TO GUESTS

Your brochure should have a dated rate schedule, any restrictions (such as minimum stays), check-in and check-out times, deposit and cancellation policies, kinds of payment accepted, house rules on pets and smoking, and any other policies that are important to you. Look at other brochures, as many as you can get, to get an idea of the kinds of things that can be included.

Many guests, however, are referred to you before they ever see your brochure. You must convey your policies to them in a way that will not be forbidding—you do want them to come! When the telephone call comes for reservations, use some policies to separate your guest from the guest who is not right for your inn (such as restrictions on smoking or small children).

Although an inn doesn't usually post its regulations on the back of a room door as motels do, we can still communicate our policies to our guests. You might use an attractive script note, nicely framed and placed on a bureau or hung on the wall. A pleasantly written welcoming letter with the guest's name on it (that helps to assure it is read) is another method. Include not only your rules, but any interesting historic tidbits about the house and the area, too.

Still another way to do this is with a room book, a nicely tabbed compendium of information about the inn, your policies, what to do in case of fire, local restaurants and attractions, and so forth. This is much more elaborate and takes quite a bit of time to create and update.

Other inns take a different approach. The innkeeper gives a tour, during which the rules are covered verbally. How you communicate your house rules depends on the type of guest you are dealing with and your price range. The higher your rates, the less appropriate are room notes.

SETTING YOUR POLICIES

Now, what sorts of policies should you have? There are situations that are so common you can't avoid them. You need the comfort of knowing how you are going to address guests who do not follow those policies. The most important ones deal with reservations, deposits, and cancellations, but there are a number of others.

Cancellations and no-shows

Every innkeeper dreads these. Inns are unlike other lodging properties: We don't overbook. The quid pro quo is: We promise a reserved guest space, and the guest promises to arrive. Well, they don't always, nor do they always understand that you can't be flexible about last-minute cancellations in the way a large property would be.

Cancellations and no-shows are often the worst for those inns in heavily touristed areas. Telling the truth and curb appeal can make a difference. If a guest feels that he or she has been lied to about what to expect, and your inn does *not* look cozy, elegant, charming, secluded, grand, or whatever epithet you've attached to it, then that guest may well drive on. And you may be out of luck.

"Make sure your cancellation policy is explicit," says Richard Carlson of Savannah's Ballastone Inn. "Guests have a million excuses for why they need to cancel on the day of arrival. Make sure you are inflexible on this rule or you will lose your shirt."

Here is a typical reservation sequence:

October 1: The guest calls and makes a reservation for the beginning of November. You pencil in the reservation and tell the guest that a deposit check must be received by mail within one week, or the reservation will be erased from the book. Send the guest a brochure.

October 6: The check arrives. You indicate this in the book.

October 7: You mail the confirmation letter to the guest (see the example below).

There are other ways of handling this sequence. Some inns (usually not those in heavy tourist areas) allow reservations to be held with a credit card number. This is similar to the way hotels hold reservations, and guests understand it. The confirmation letters should go out to these guests at once.

When there is time, you should send a brochure or introductory letter to the guest, reiterating your important policies. If you require an advance deposit by check or money order a certain time before the reservation date, state that policy. You can do so pleasantly, but do it.

Here's an example of a confirmation letter that, with the appropriate alterations, can serve as an introductory letter or a confirmation:

Dear,

We're looking forward to welcoming you to Scratch Inn for the three nights of October 2, 3, and 4. We've reserved a room with a queen-sized bed and private bath at $80 per night. We'll do all we can to make your anniversary celebration special. Your planned arrival time of 6 P.M. is fine; if you expect to arrive at a different time, please let us know so that your room can be ready.

We will expect your deposit check of $120 (50 percent of the total amount) by September 15, or we cannot hold the accommodation. [*Alternate:* Your reservation is confirmed by your credit card number.] If unexpected circumstances require you to cancel, we must receive notice of the cancellation by 2 P.M., September 29. We will return your deposit [*or:* We will issue a credit slip] even if your cancellation is later if we are able to rebook the room. Please be reminded that we do not permit smoking at Scratch Inn.

We serve afternoon tea to all the guests at 5 P.M. each day. We always have an interesting group of guests, and many friendships have been made here. If you have any questions, the enclosed brochure will answer many of them, but don't hesitate to call if others occur to you.

Such a latter makes it clear that the deposit must be held in the event of a cancellation. Your inn's policies on how much of the deposit to return or whether to charge for only one night, will vary. I think you should return the entire deposit if you are able to rebook the room; it creates some goodwill when there is a genuinely good reason for cancellation.

Carl, however, strongly disagrees, as do many other innkeepers. He believes in assessing a $5 to $10 handling charge, no matter what the reason, to cover your innkeeping expenses. Some inns do not refund the deposit, and instead apply it to a future date.

Brochures are a good place to state how you handle refunds. Here is how the brochure of Sunny Pines Bed & Breakfast in Harwich West, Massachusetts, does it:

1. Deposit must be received within one week from when you call to make a reservation.

2. Entire amount is requested for stays of less than seven nights, one-half payment for longer stays. The deposit then applies to last days with balance due payable upon arrival.

3. Deposit will be happily refunded or applied to a new date if the cancellation is received two weeks prior to arrival date. If not, we will do our best to fill your room, and if successful, we will return your deposit. No refund on early departure. Ten percent service charge for credit card cancellations.

4. Your canceled check or credit card slip is your receipt.

The really tough situation is when the guest cancels on the check-in day because of an illness or accident. That's no problem if you're able to rebook to a walk-in, but you can't count on it. You'll have to consult your own soft-heartedness, but consider that you and your inn deserve not to be sacrificed to the whim, or even misfortunes, of a guest. Remember what Richard Carlson says about losing your shirt.

No-shows are the most awful experience for innkeepers. Until it happens to you, you cannot imagine how bad it is. Why? If you have only five rooms, and two couples don't show up, you've just lost 40 percent of your revenue for that day! This perishable commodity cannot be recovered. So you sit and wait for hours, wondering what happened and why and what to do.

If you collected a deposit, it's not a total loss. If you don't have that, you can try sending out a bill. Good luck on collecting. If someone is ill-mannered enough not to show up without an explanation, what likelihood is there that he will pay any attention to a bill?

One other way to deal with no-shows is to use a credit card guarantee. Some companies (and banks) are better about this than others. We believe that card companies are too willing to charge back to the inn on the mere word of a guest. After all, they want to keep the card holder as *their* customer. You should always find out what the policy is for Visa and MasterCard through the bank you intend to use. If you follow its rules, the bank should be willing to extend the guarantee. If not, look for another bank. American Express and Discover will also issue the guarantee.

If a guest cancels without enough notice but has reserved the room with a credit card number, issue that guest a cancellation number, and write it on the cancelled reservation. You make the number up, so it doesn't matter what the number is as long as you keep a record of it. If you then charge the guest because the room was not rebooked and the guest refuses the charge, you can ask the credit card company if the guest used that cancellation number. If the guest did, then you have proof that the guest in fact made the reservation. It's a wee bit of trickery, but it's a legitimate weapon against the inconsiderate types who make your life miserable. If your cancellation policy is clear and you have made a practice of tracking in this way—and if it doesn't happen very often—you have some leverage with the card companies.

Another method is to charge the guest when he makes the reservation. The credit card companies now have these little gizmos that allow you to run a credit card number through and get the money immediately. If the charge is refused, you may still have a problem.

If you don't accept credit cards, you have no way to guarantee last-minute reservations, when there is no time to receive a deposit. If that reservation doesn't show, you're out of luck. Even the smallest inns should take some cards. It is also worth noting that if you want business travelers, you'll almost certainly have to accept the inconvenience of American Express.

Asking for your money

Innkeepers are at first sometimes a bit shy about asking for payment. Some advisers say you should always expect payment on check-in. In most cases that is a good idea.

Your ambience, again, will dictate what you do. If you want your guests to feel like friends on a visit, you might prefer payment on checkout. Guests often feel more comfortable about paying then, especially when their stay has been pleasant.

On the other hand, there are those rare occasions when someone walks out without paying. This happens mostly in homestays and smaller B&Bs.

Children

Children around an inn can be your own or your guests'. One of the demographic trends of the 1990s is older couples with children. These couples like to do things as a family, creating a ticklish problem for innkeepers.

Most inn-goers will not be happy in an inn where there are children. Yet if you systematically exclude children, you may run afoul of laws protecting the civil rights of minorities (yes, children are people, too). Many innkeepers are becoming concerned with this possibility.

It is not an easy dilemma to resolve, but there are solutions. Once again, you must come back to what kind of inn you are trying to create and how you convey that to potential guests.

First of all, there is business—quite a lot, we think—to be gained from accepting children, if you can manage it well.

Make it clear in your brochure with a line that says "Children welcome." Potential guests will be alerted that there may be children in residence, and they can make plans accordingly. Inns that accept families have to make sure they have such things as cribs, rollaway cots for the parents' rooms, and childproof sleeping and public rooms. Fred Strout of Applewood Colonial Inn in Williamsburg, Virginia, even offers babysitting services to guests.

But what about those many inns that present themselves as romantic retreats? Their ambience (and much of their business) would be destroyed if they accepted children.

If you are not an inn that can deal with children, you need to let people know that: "The inn is not suitable for small children," or "The inn has no activities for children," or "Small children find us boring." Such statements will put families on notice that your inn may not be appropriate for them. Or you can state quite frankly that children are incompatible with your ambience, as Seacrest Manor does: "For the comfort of our guests, and as our accommodations are limited, we cannot accept reservations for children under 16 or for groups."

The tone of your brochure should convey whether you are suitable for children. Mentioning antiques (please don't say "antique-filled") will often tip travelers off.

Pricing will also serve to encourage or discourage children. If you make no distinction in rates for children and adults, guests are on reasonable notice that you are not family-oriented. You may also say "only two persons per room." If people are traveling with a child, they will have to book two rooms, and the cost would be prohibitive to most families.

The travel guidebooks are excellent about letting their readers know whether you are child-friendly.

Finally, people are usually good about asking if children are welcome when they call for reservations. You should be honest in your response.

Let me digress for a moment into the area of discrimination and civil rights. Smaller properties are unlikely to face lawsuits charging them with discrimination. It is an extremely rare person who feels he must sue on a matter of principle. Such a person would have to be determined to bring a child to an inn—and it's far cheaper to get a babysitter for one weekend. Courts will avoid such cases, because they know you have to be able to create the kind of business that will bring in income. You are not required to destroy your own living.

You would not, of course, want it to go so far. There probably is such a person out there, but all you can do to protect yourself is take reasonable precautions. The reasonable precaution in this case is to avoid putting a line in your brochure that says "We don't take children." The AB&BA also advises against outright bans; discourage children if your inn is not appropriate.

There was a time when children did travel well. And there are many children who still do. As Dinie says, "There are no bad children, only bad parents." Some parents create problems for all families when they fail to notice or deal with the disturbances their children create for others. Alas, many innkeepers have gotten stuck baby-sitting, as thoughtless parents dump their children and escape for an afternoon or evening. This is not part of the deal, and innkeepers should firmly refuse such responsibilities (if for no other reason than the insurance considerations). If you do get stuck, at least add a babysitting charge.

Most innkeepers will accept children on a slow night. If a parent really wants to bring a child to your inn, you might suggest a midweek visit in the slow season. Dinie says this is our chance "to educate the next generation of inn-goers"—an idea we all need to take under advisement. Children are often delightful guests. You cannot predict their behavior any more than you can an adult guest's. I can remember one who wanted to bring her nine-year-old daughter. I was skeptical, but the parent said, "Oh, she's better behaved than I am!" The little girl was a pleasure. She enjoyed the house and never disturbed the other guests. The best solution, I think, is to set rules that apply to *all* guests, regardless of age: No running, loud parties, disturbing other guests, destroying inn property, and so forth. If anyone, of any age, breaks your rules, out they go. You are then enforcing *behavior,* not discriminating because of age.

Pets

For a number of reasons, most inns cannot accept pets. I find this unfortunate, since pets can be pleasant traveling companions. I must admit I've always liked the way many Europeans take their pets along on trips. It is not against French or English restaurant health codes to allow animals in dining rooms. In these countries, one often sees a diner with his dog under the table.

American health departments frown on this practice, and American pet owners often make matters worse by not training their pets properly and by not keeping them free of pests. This makes for trouble for inn owners who would like to accept pets. Cats with their claws can ruin your linens, draperies, and upholstery. Cats or dogs with fleas can bring an infestation to your inn that will plague you, your pets, and future guests for months. Pets with urinary problems (or poor house training) can be even more destructive.

Another serious problem is allergies. Many guests are allergic to animal hair, particularly cat hair. It isn't fair to make them miserable because there are pets around. For this reason, if you have pets of your own, keep them out of guest rooms. If you aren't going to enforce this, make sure your guests understand that.

There are also guests with phobias about certain kinds of animals. We have had guests who were afraid of our pets, and we had to take care to keep them apart. These fears are irrational; there's no point in arguing about them. You do not want an unhappy guest, so your pets—who are wonderfully entertaining to most guests—must be out of sight of people who fear them.

If you do have pets of your own, they may be an additional reason to keep guests' pets out of your inn. Established animals don't always take well to newcomers. Friends have brought their dogs, which always entertained our dog, Jeff, cheerfully in their own homes, to the inn. On his territory, however, these dogs behaved aggressively toward Jeff. This is part of the vicious circle: Because Americans don't travel often with their pets, their pets often don't travel well.

The simplest policy is to put "pets not accepted" in your brochure and handle specific cases as they come up. You can offer to find a place at a nearby kennel for the animals. If you find yourself dealing with many pets, you may be able to negotiate a special rate at a particular kennel in exchange for sending all your guests' pets there. If guests bring their cats in cages—and promise to keep them there—you might allow them in the rooms. (Of course, keep in mind that the owners might break their promises.)

Check-in and check-out times

These are not trivial matters. You cannot always be in the inn, and you may not always have an assistant there. You have to have some time to clean rooms, attend meetings, make in-person marketing visits, shop for supplies, go to the bank or post office, or any of a number of other things that have to be done to keep your inn running.

A single innkeeper like Judy Studer at Flemington's Jerica Hill has a very restrictive check-in period (4 to 7 P.M.). She has no staff, and, in addition to running the five-room B&B, is active in the community and has two children. "It *is* possible to be SuperMom. I just have to schedule my time very tightly, especially when new guests are scheduled to arrive."

If you allow guests to check in at any time, you'll find yourself with the previous night's guests still visiting with you or one another, unprepared rooms, and no hope of getting it all organized.

You must manage the flow of traffic through your inn in order to operate efficiently. If you don't, you'll seem harried, and you'll spoil the ambience. The fault will be all your own. The next stage is innkeeper burnout.

Allow yourself a minimum of half an hour per room for cleaning. If you have eight rooms, you should allow four hours between regular checkout and check-in. That way, if your maids decide not to show and you have to change the whole house, you can get it done in time for your next set of guests.

With any luck this will never happen, but innkeepers can count on Murphy's Law and all of its corollaries. Be quite strict about this policy, because guests will say they want to check in at certain times without really meaning it. You might on occasion allow a noon check-in, only to find yourself waiting around for hours for a guest who doesn't arrive until 4 P.M. That sort of thing can put you in a bad mood, and you're not likely to be a good host if you're in a bad mood.

Smoking

Even as late as 1987 it was rather daring to forbid smoking. Now it is easier. Since only 30 percent of the population smokes, 70 percent of your potential guests prefer to be in a nonsmoking environment.

For safety, health, and maintenance reasons, most inns today are nonsmoking, and most guests expect it. Nevertheless, there are guests who do smoke, and these are often hard-core, unrepentant smokers. Put your smoking policy in your brochure, and state it on the phone. It doesn't hurt to put signs in each room that say "Thank you for not smoking."

Let guests know this policy early. At Wedgwood, after the availability of a requested date is confirmed, the next information given is that the inn is nonsmoking. Weed them out early; why go through the entire reservation spiel for nothing?

There will be the occasional guest who will break your rule. All you can do is keep track of who did it (and you will know), and make sure you do not allow that guest to return.

If you allow smoking, you should let nonsmokers know. You could also set aside nonsmoking rooms, and certainly a nonsmoking sitting area.

Breakfast times

Inns serve breakfast in many different ways and at many different times. Some serve everyone together at a fixed time. Some set a range of times for breakfast service. Some serve breakfast in bed or put trays outside the room. Some serve coffee and pastries quite late. Much depends on what you can do and what you're trying to accomplish in the way of ambience.

You should make quite clear how you do your breakfasts and what you expect of guests. Because she cannot seat everyone at once, Margaret Perry of the Thomas Shepherd Inn has her guests sign up for a particular time the night before.

Other innkeepers have guests sign up for when they want tray delivery to their rooms. Some inns have specialties that are timed and cannot be kept warm. Guests are informed that the time is not flexible, but that the breakfast is worth the trouble of being there at a particular time.

Public and private space

You need to make clear to guests where they may freely roam. The inn is your home, and you ought to keep some parts of it to yourself no matter how generous you are.

King's Cottage has a nice little sign: "Please respect closed doors." That covers several bases. Guests often want to look at other rooms, but you can't have them walking in on other guests!

Some innkeepers are happy to have guests in their kitchens and may even invite them in. Others don't like it. If you're one of the latter, put a "private" or "please knock" sign on the door.

Few guests will abuse these rules; the one who does should be politely but firmly corrected: "I'm sorry. Guests are not allowed in this area. If you'll step into the parlor, I'll be glad to take care of any request." Of course, you need to make it possible for guests to find you easily so that they aren't inclined to go poking into areas they should stay out of.

Tea and afternoon refreshments

Serving your guests beverages or light snacks in the late afternoon provides an opportunity for your guests to get to know you and each other. It also gives you a chance to try your culinary skills on something other than breakfast.

Should you provide alcoholic beverages? Generally not. There are liability consequences, and there might be local ordinances that don't permit it. Providing drinks can be quite expensive, so keep that in mind, as well.

Guests often bring their own alcohol or food. They may want to keep their provisions in your refrigerator. How you handle this is up to you. You may refuse to allow them to bring these into your inn, or you may restrict where they can take their goodies. People eating in their rooms will cause cleaning problems. Many guests won't ask your permission; they'll just do it.

Afternoon tea and refreshments is one way of heading off the in-room gourmand. If you feed them a snack yourself, they'll be less likely to sneak one later in their rooms.

Tipping

As you add staff, this becomes a ticklish question. A few guests do leave tips in the room as a matter of course, and they are often generous ones. But most guests do not.

In the Northeast, encouraging tipping is one way to get the kind of chamber help you need. The further south and west you go, the less problem there seems to be.

Encouraging tipping, however, may lead to a potential clash with guests. If you leave an envelope for tips in the room, they will feel they are being charged something that they weren't told about. On the other hand, without that extra income for the

cleaners you may end up on the thin edge of profitability—
things can be that tight.

One solution is to include the service charge on the bill.
Many upscale inns are doing this. The gratuity is added on just
as the sales tax is. Handling it that way seems to cause less of-
fense.

Seacrest Manor puts an attractive card in the rooms that
reads: "Many of our guests have suggested that it is less confusing and fairer to add the gratuities to the bill. Therefore, a
charge of ten percent of the basic room rate will be included on
your bill and distributed to the appropriate staff members." By
putting the suggestion at the door of previous guests and by
making the issue one of fairness, Leighton Saville and Dwight
MacCormack have headed off potential complaints.

---◆---

8

Attention to Detail: No Inn Is Great Without It

"In this business, an innkeeper who is not organized is done for."

—Annette King

Good innkeeping is in the details and how you handle them. How *many* details you will come to appreciate as you go along. You can get lost in the details or you can use them to make your inn's statement (something, that larger lodging properties cannot do). And although no detail is unimportant, some are more so than others.

Of them all, the most important is cleanliness. Says Helen Goodbrod of Ye Olde Library Bed & Breakfast in Jersey Shore, Pennsylvania, "Details in innkeeping that are most essential are a clean home, clean bed linens, lots of clean towels, and air conditioning in the summertime."

Reasonable warmth in the winter, with lots of quilts and blankets for snuggling on chilly nights, is also expected. Guests like to read in bed, so there should be good lighting (at least 100 watts) on both sides.

Private baths are no longer considered an amenity. Edward Mahoney, a tourist extension specialist at Michigan State University, led a university-funded study of B&B clientele in Michigan. A major conclusion of the study was that most guests who shared a bathroom would have preferred a private one. Most guests who had private baths said they would not have stayed in a B&B if the room had not had one. Most guests also said they would pay extra for a private bath.

But much of the detail in inns isn't what you provide; it's how you provide it. Knowing what you want to offer and what kinds of guests will help you stay on top of the details that will make your inn successful.

THE TELEPHONE

Peg McCabe of the Queen Anne Inn in Newport, Rhode Island, says that good telephone skills are essential to operating a successful inn. "I spend a lot of money in ads and direct mail to generate telephone calls from prospective guests. To ensure that that money's well spent I answer the phone promptly and at all hours. I can also 'read' people over the phone, weeding out those callers I think wouldn't like what my inn offers."

Dinie at Wedgwood agrees. "Callers have told me I have the ability to 'smile over the phone' and establish an easy rapport with them. I have never tried to convert a Holiday Inn-goer to our B&B. If a prospective guest really wants an in-room television or whirlpool bath, I refer that caller elsewhere. We only want happy guests at our inn. Being able to discern their needs and wants over the telephone is critical in screening out those who would be unhappy."

Inns cannot afford to let telephone callers slip away. Except for drop-in business, all initial guest contacts are over the phone. Unless you have an 800 number, it's the caller's dime; you should be willing to spend as much time on the phone as they are. Here are some useful telephone tips.

• Answer the telephone within the first three rings. Your voice should be pleasant, conveying a genuine interest in assisting the caller; the first 30 seconds are the most important in making an impression.

• You should demonstrate knowledge of the product or service. After a greeting, identify yourself as the innkeeper and give your name.

• Take a slow, deep breath before you answer the phone. This will help you speak slowly and clearly. Smile as you answer; somehow that smile projects itself through the line.

• Be a reservation-taker, not just an information-giver. Try to find out exactly what the caller is looking for; don't just give facts about the inn.

• Keep the conversation flowing, especially while you look up information.

• Never leave a caller on hold for long periods.

• Address the caller by name, if he or she gives it to you.

• Offer alternatives—such as alternate dates or referrals to other inns—if you cannot meet the caller's needs.

• Repeat any information you gather for clarity and completeness.

• Return calls and messages as soon as possible.

Answering machines

An answering machine can be a godsend to the harried innkeeper, if used properly. But many callers hate them; the machines make them feel self-conscious. They may also feel they are being treated impersonally (the last impression you want them to have). So how do you overcome these problems?

First of all, don't feel guilty. If you are a small property, you cannot afford to be on call 24 hours a day. You can't afford it in wear and tear on yourself, and you can't afford an all-night desk clerk. Potential guests who think you accept reservations at 3 A.M. are not guests you want anyway.

There are right ways to use the answering machine, however. The message should be clear, and there should be sufficient time for a potential guest to leave a message. Nothing is more irritating than to be cut off in mid-message. Since there is the possibility that a guest is calling at 3 A.M. because of an emergency, the message should include an emergency number for off hours.

I discovered that the answering machine I had bought for Boydville had a fifteen-minute outgoing message tape. It also had a feature that allowed the caller to push a button to end the outgoing message and begin his own. Putting these two facts together, I decided to put a *very* long and complete description of the inn on the outgoing message, beginning with "You may interrupt this tape and leave a message by pressing the asterisk on your phone." I also indicated how long the message was—five minutes! Some guests have called back to listen to the message several times. It made them more comfortable about making reservations (there are, believe it or not, many people who are nervous about calling for reservations).

An 800 number? A fax machine?

Innkeepers who have them say that 800 numbers do encourage calls. They are not overwhelmingly expensive (as opposed to a WATS line, which is), and will get you calls from travel agents who won't call an inn without an 800 number. Even the smallest inn can consider one of these.

Fax machines are becoming as common as telephones. If you are trying to encourage bookings from the business traveler or corporate client, then a fax machine is a must for their business communication. You will also find fax machines useful for travel agent confirmations and standard reservation forms.

ANSWERING THE MAIL

Speed in responding to written communications is essential. Says Leighton Saville: "Twenty minutes after our mail is delivered the postal truck swings past our house again to deliver to the other side of the street. We try to answer our guest mail fast enough to have it ready for that returning mail truck. Not only is the speedy handling of our mail appreciated by our guests, but it also helps us obtain new business by being the first to respond to a prospective guest's inquiry. It may be a small detail, but it counts."

AMENITIES

Amenities are part and parcel of inn-going. A true amenity goes beyond what is expected of any good room. Amenities do *not* include mirrors in the bathrooms, good reading lights, comfortable chairs, comfortable beds, blankets, closets, a sitting room for guests. You ought to have these things, and you should not consider them amenities.

Amenities are surprises: nice soaps, unusually large and fluffy towels, bathrobes, afternoon tea, fresh flowers, fresh fruit, games in the public sitting room, books and magazines, and so on. Guests have come to expect some little amenities—the more expensive the inn, the more they expect them—and innkeepers delight in providing them. Here are the amenities provided by some inns:

Deb and Gary Leitner, Hillside Farm, Lancaster County, Pennsylvania: "Smoke-free rooms; first floor rooms for the handicapped; soap, shampoo, and other bath products in the bathrooms; *large* fluffy towels; extra blankets in the rooms; bathrobes in closets of rooms with shared baths; clocks in each room; separate thermostats for each room; ceiling fans in each room; magazines and books in each room; games, puzzles, and TV in the common area; rocking chairs on the porch; cold spring water in each room; refrigerator for guest use; special items for anniversary, birthday, or honeymoon guests."

Mae McQuade, Split-Pine Farmhouse, Pine Grove Mills, Pennsylvania: "Hampers of sodas and buckets of ice in the upstairs hallways; lovely glasses on the servers; cordials and small glasses in each room; very special soaps; tea or coffee for weary travelers; potpourri and flowers from my garden."

Richard Carlson, Ballastone Inn, Savannah: "Full-service bar, courtyard, elevators, turn-down service, free off-street parking, public spaces, fireplaces, Jacuzzis."

Guests are more likely to pay extra for in-room (private) amenities, such as Jacuzzis, fireplaces, views, balconies, oversized beds, than they are for public amenities like acreage, walking trails, or extra sitting rooms. This means more private amenities can yield greater income.

A few words of caution about Jacuzzis, hot tubs, and fireplaces: These can be dangerous items for guests or for your house. Make sure that they are not set up dangerously and that your guests know how to use them. Gas fireplaces with timers are not a bad solution. In any case, they are easier to deal with and safer than wood-burning ones. Guests don't have to get out of bed to feed them, and they don't leave an unfortunate smell behind. If you deal with wood-burning fireplaces much, you quickly understand why our ancestors closed them up and went to central heating. Be very careful about hot tubs. Make the rules clear—no pregnant women or unsupervised young children. Hyperthermia can kill. Hot tubs are also difficult to keep clean, and soap scum can transfer diseases. For these reasons, we do not recommend these appliances be installed.

Bar service, too, can cause liability problems. Make sure your insurance covers it. Fewer guests are drinking heavily these days, and you can easily get by without serving liquor. Homemade liqueurs, however, are a nice touch.

One final word about liquor: One reason drinking is down is because more people are recovering alcoholics. Do not be insistent about offering alcohol because you may be tempting a guest unkindly.

Afternoon tea or refreshments are increasingly becoming an expected amenity at inns. In any season an appropriate non-alcoholic beverage is appreciated: iced tea with mint from your garden in summer, hot apple cider with a cinnamon stick in winter. Guests will appreciate being offered something late in the afternoon after a long day of driving or sightseeing.

Offering food is a time-honored way of saying welcome, and we recommend it. As Dinie says, low-cost, simple, yet thoughtful amenities, such as a plate of home-baked cookies or a bowl of fruit in the common room, are often the most appreciated. If you serve a more elaborate tea, most innkeepers will recommend that you set the time with guests. That way you won't be fixing tea or washing glasses all day long. Finally, getting all the guests together at once with a cup or glass helps lubricate the social interaction that characterizes inns at their best.

Turn-down service is a matter of controversy. I've never felt comfortable doing it; it seems to me to be an invasion of a guest's privacy. And, as a business traveler on the road, I always found it silly to see my spread turned back and a chocolate on the pillow. Why would I want chocolate at that time of the night? Don't do a turn-down service—or any other amenity—if you think it's silly. It won't be you and therefore will violate the principles of good innkeeping.

On the other hand, if you like doing a turn-down service and you think it adds a special touch, by all means do it, and put a mint or a flower or an embroidered take-home gift on the pillow. It offers you a chance to put a room to rights and to put in fresh towels. This is much appreciated. If you don't do the service, then you need to put extra towels in the room or in some convenient place. Lesley Hubbard at the Victoria and Albert Inn in Abingdon, Virginia, puts huge baskets of fluffy towels in her shared baths—a beautiful and thoughtful touch. There must be twenty towels in each of those baskets.

Some amenities you offer will depend on your area. Ski lockers or bicycles are useful in some. Others offer golfing privileges (or swimming privileges) at nearby resorts or country clubs. Anything that extends what your inn's offering could be considered an amenity. Each will say that you are a thoughtful, caring host and that you go far beyond what a hotel or motel would do.

One of the most important amenities you can provide is to share what you know about your area. If you are a good tour guide, you can make sure your guests have a good time. Use this as a way to suggest to your guests that there is so much more to do in your area than they can hope to cover in one visit. This will encourage them to return.

Historic inns offer tours of the house. Telling stories about its history or its decorations often delights guests. Of course, there are guests who say, "Skip the tour; just show me my room."

Is a guest telephone an amenity? Less so than it used to be. An extra phone with a separate number (so the inn's line isn't kept busy) is not a major expense. If you do not designate a long-distance carrier, guests can use their credit cards or call collect. That way you won't have to worry about someone putting large charges on your bill.

Modern technology now makes providing in-room telephones, or a semblance of them, relatively easy. If you have a second number, you can buy a "base" station that plugs into your electrical wiring and a "satellite" plug that can be put in any room in the house, creating a telephone jack there. Guests can take the inn phone into their rooms. You need to keep people from abusing that privilege. You might put the phone in a basket, with a note asking them to return it to the basket when they are finished.

In-room TVs are not an expected amenity. Perhaps they will become one, though we have found that guests at inns are not couch-potato types. You must really have a TV in the public room, because television has become a sort of shared public space of its own. Wives will often go out shopping, leaving their husbands to enjoy a football game. Sometimes, if you arrange this unobtrusively, both halves of the couple will thank you. (In order not to be accused of sexism, we'll acknowledge the existence of football-watching wives and shopping husbands, though they are not in the majority.) Anyway, try to accommodate everyone.

Special soaps and other bathroom amenities are becoming cliché, as even low-end hotels offer them. You can do a little extra advertising if you put your inn's logo and phone number on them. Guests often like to buy a box of soaps to take home; some inns pay for their soaps with these sales. You might consider adding a few items to the usual soap and shampoo found in guest bathrooms: glycerine soap for those with sensitive skin, shoe mitts (these will discourage guests from using your washcloths to polish shoes), shower caps, a mending kit, hand lotion, bubble bath, cologne, or after-shave lotion. The soap suppliers have long lists of additional items, some of which are silly. But you might want to put in a small supply of extra toothbrushes and toothpaste, disposable razors, shaving cream, and any other item that might be forgotten. Calls for these are not frequent, but having them on hand shows you are especially thoughtful.

Fresh flowers in rooms or in the common area do show thoughtfulness to your guests, but they are, in many areas, very expensive—prohibitively so in certain seasons. Green plants are also nice and last longer, but they require watering, which is easy to forget in the haste of changing rooms from one guest to another.

In general, balance your rates, costs, and occupancy to decide how far you will go with amenities. The costs can mount quickly. You could easily spend $40 to $50 per guest room on amenities if you went whole hog. If your rates are high enough, they may justify (or require) that expense. But don't start out with more than you can easily manage because you rarely subtract amenities.

RESERVATION FORMS AND BOOKS

If you don't keep careful track of reservations, you won't be in the business long. There are successful innkeepers who still do not have a reservation book, but we suspect they are successful in spite of themselves.

Professionally run inns have separate forms or slips for each guest. The information requested on the form should have a purpose so that you don't hold people on the phone unnecessarily. The following information should be included on the form:

current date
dates of reservation
guest name
address
day and evening telephone numbers
room assigned
room rate quoted (sometimes you give discounts)
credit card number (if appropriate)

date deposit is due (if appropriate)
how the guest was referred to you
time of arrival
notes

All of this information is important to you. You might also keep your payment records on the reservation form. After you have acknowledged the reservation with a confirmation letter, you should file the slip by scheduled date of arrival. The simplest method is a file box with month dividers, and in the current month, day dividers. Keep moving the current day divider to the next month, rearranging future cards as you go.

Once made, reservations must be penciled into the reservation book, or *booked*. This can be as simple as a customized week-at-a-glance calendar, or it can be more complex, with space to note the deposit was received and the time of arrival. I find the latter essential on the book. It allows me to see at once who is coming when, and I can plan greetings accordingly.

Financially successful inns spend a lot of thought on how to take reservations, with the goal to book as many room nights as possible. The strategy? Use policies such as minimum length of stay to piece together your reservation book puzzle.

For example, a six-room urban inn shouldn't book all its available rooms for a weekday night with only single-night stays. They know from previous experience that there is a good chance a business person will call closer to the date, requesting a multiple-night stay. Similarly, a college inn with strong weekend business does not want to book the whole house for only one weekend night if Monday is a legal holiday. It's very likely to receive requests for three-night stays for that weekend.

The sample from a reservation book shown on page 116 has the rooms arranged vertically, but you can as easily arrange them horizontally and the days vertically. This particular reservation form is on my computer. I print it out as needed, punch holes in it, and put it into a three-ring notebook with page dividers for the month.

You can buy reservation books or make up your own. Drawing yours first by hand and then photocopying it will work fine. Or you can set it up on a computer and print out pages as needed.

Some innkeepers suggest that you keep a second, easily portable, week-at-a-glance reservation book that merely notes

Month:

Date	Sun	Mon	Tues	Wed	Thu	Fri	Sat
Blue Room							
Guest							
Arr. Time							
Deposit							
Notes							
Red Room							
Guest							
Arr. Time							
Deposit							
Notes							
Green Room							
Guest							
Arr. Time							
Deposit							
Notes							
Maple Suite							
Guest							
Arr. Time							
Deposit							
Notes							
Elm Suite							
Guest							
Arr. Time							
Deposit							
Notes							
Chestnut Room							
Guest							
Arr. Time							
Deposit							
Notes							

occupancy so that you can take reservations on the run. You have to decide what fits your style and degree of organization.

Sally Blumberg of Sunday's Mill Farm in Bernville, Pennsylvania, is supremely well organized: "I have found it important to have a separate calendar for reservations. I have an information card on each guest so that I can record dates of all calls, brochure and confirmation mailings, and check numbers. I even take a photo of my guests to help me remember them when they call for later reservations."

After the guest's stay, the reservation cards or forms should be filed alphabetically. This will give you a handy guest list for newsletter mailings. If you are really organized, you might jot down pertinent details about the guest so that you will be more easily able to remember their likes and dislikes when they return. When a returning guest who you noted "especially liked the hazelnut souffle" is served it again with a comment like, "I hope you enjoy this as much the second time," the impression you leave is invaluable. No hotel can do that.

A card file with sections for gift certificates, postponements, and your "A" list (yes, you will find yourself rating your guests) is also useful.

Care is the hallmark of the innkeeper; keeping detailed guest records is but another example of that care. You should think enough of your guests to try to remember them. It takes effort, but that effort is appreciated.

HOUSEKEEPING AND MAINTENANCE

You are not only running an inn, you are also managing a large property that needs regular upkeep. Guests cause wear and tear on your house (not as much as full-time live-in family), but they don't expect the wear and tear to show. Standards are higher for an inn than for a private home. At home, guests live with half-used soap and toilet paper and frayed towels, but they expect better from an inn.

Here's a look at what your home can expect from temporary residents: nicks and scrapes from large suitcases bumping against walls and furniture, stopped-up toilets, window shades knocked askew, scratched and worn floors and carpets from considerable traffic in entrance areas and public areas, worn mattresses (some of your guests will be quite large), chipped china, broken glasses, stained napkins. Your linens will also wear out surprisingly quickly. (Because of frequent washing, towels may last no more than four months, no matter how good the quality.)

Carol Ringoot, former innkeeper at the Thomas Shepherd Inn, says that she was always astonished at how many light bulbs she needed. You will be, too; you're keeping more lights on longer for the safety and comfort of your guests. And you will use *lots* of toilet paper (we have no idea what guests do with it all).

You should have a basic complement of tools and hardware—screwdrivers and extra screws, hammer, pliers, furniture glue, etc. They should be easy to find and kept in working order. Take care of small items as you go. Towel bars, which come loose as people yank towels off, need to be tightened; luggage racks and chairs need regluing.

The following suggestions are just a sample of the routine maintenance that gives your equipment and furniture a longer life:

- Get maintenance contracts on major appliances and house components.
- Put "egg-crate" foam pads between the mattress and box spring.
- Use mattress covers on all mattresses and pillow ticks or covers on the pillows.
- Turn the mattresses regularly (at least every quarter) and vacuum them.
- Set up a painting schedule. For example, paint one-quarter of the interior each year so that by the end of four years you've redone the entire house.
- Replace filters on air conditioners and furnaces before every season.
- Have wood-burning chimneys swept each season and clean out the gutters.

Get in the habit of doing something fairly regularly. The more you do, the more you'll see. We do maintenance seasonally, anticipating what needs to be done by several weeks. Most innkeepers learn this the hard way—when the snow arrives is not the time to be outside putting up storm windows. As with everything else, scheduling is everything. You have to think ahead.

Even if the house is empty, you need to keep on top of the housekeeping. A rotating schedule of cleaning is a good idea: freshen the rooms between guests, and do a good cleaning weekly, at the least. Always change towels every day and sheets every other day (some wait until the third day, but we think that is too long).

You will have to train your staff to make the beds the way *you* want them made. This is not as simple as you might think. You don't want the bed made army-style, with everything tucked in tightly.

Owen says that all the little things together make the room special: fringes on oriental rugs straight, window shades even, towels neatly arranged on the towel bars, pillows plumped, spreads even, dust ruffles neatly pleated, and so on.

RECORDKEEPING

You must keep good records if for no other reason than tax purposes. If you really hate bookkeeping—and I know very few people who like it—then make it as easy on yourself as possible. Put all your bills in one place. Record the amounts and descriptions of all payments in your checkbook. Record all receipts from your guests. Then each quarter give everything to your bookkeeper or accountant.

Note that we said to record *all* receipts from your guests. We know that some restaurants and inns pocket cash receipts without recording them so as to avoid paying sales and income taxes. Do not do this! Not only is it dishonest, but it will also work to your disadvantage in the long run.

Suppose you get about six years down the road. You are doing a good business—perhaps 50 percent occupancy—and are pocketing a few thousand a month. You decide to sell your thriving business, but your books show you grossing about $10,000 less than you really are. The value of your business is usually figured as a multiple of gross receipts. As a result your selling price may be tens of thousands of dollars less than its value because you cannot prove you took in that money. Worse, if you tell the potential buyer that you have been skimming the profits, that buyer is going to wonder about your honesty in other areas.

Paper systems

Although you don't want to be an accountant, you will probably be taking in the receipts and paying the bills yourself. There are lots of ways of doing this, but the best paper accounting system is a "one-write" pegboard.

If you've never used one, here's how it works: Checks are arranged in a layered series, with carbon strips under the payee line. Thus, when you write a check, the same information goes directly onto your bookkeeping page underneath. When you get to the bottom of the page, you total the columns and carry over to the next page. The same is true of receipts.

One-write systems are widely available at office supply stores, through your bank or accountant, or through the Professional Association of Innkeepers International, if you join.

The computer in the inn

Computers are a love-hate thing. Here you are hearing from innkeepers on both sides: Carl hates them; I like them. Even from my viewpoint, however, I would say small inns can't make really efficient use of computers unless one of the partners is already reasonably computer literate.

If you have more than eight rooms, however, you'll find them to be very useful. Also, if you want to do your own bookkeeping and accounting to save some money, the computer is indispensable.

One issue that worries innkeepers is whether a computer makes their inns less personal. The short answer is no. Computers are an extension of your abilities—a tool and nothing more. In the hands of a bureaucrat, computers reinforce bureaucratic impersonality. In the hands of a caring innkeeper, computers perform dozens of tasks, freeing the innkeeper for the more personal aspects of innkeeping. They allow you to keep better track of your guests and their likes and dislikes. They can also help keep your inn afloat by giving you early warning of problems.

Let's assume that you're acquainted with computers in general but don't have much firsthand experience. Without telling you a lot about how they work (there are good books on the subject), I can tell you roughly how they can fit into an inn.

Computers are excellent for keeping records, doing calculations, and speeding up repetitive tasks. They are ideal for accounting, preparing mass mailings, and searching guest records (if you have been faithful about entering them) for useful combinations of information.

Because there are so many different tasks you can use the computer for, you will have to have several programs to do them: a database (for guest lists), a word processing program, an accounting program (for bookkeeping), and perhaps a spreadsheet (if you want to do pretty pictures of your occupancy rate).

It does get fascinating, and if you're not careful, the computer monster can swallow you. Don't think you can do everything with a computer. Carl's excellent advice is to subcontract certain functions to a computer service: word processing, guest record files, and mass mailings (when your list gets large enough). Save your computer time for accounting. You can make good use of a machine that keeps daily records with a few keystrokes instead of letting you pile up receipts until they need an expensive accountant's time to straighten them out.

But suppose you want to do more with your new toy? There are some good innkeeping programs that will handle your reservations and deposits and mail out confirmations. I do not know (at least at this writing) of a system that combines reservations with full accounting, guest records, and mailings.

The good innkeeper programs do combine some basic bookkeeping with guest records and reservations, and some have the capacity to do response letters. At this writing, these are Front Desk, InnSoft, InnPal, and MacInn (addresses and numbers are easily available in the *Inn Review Yellow Pages*). You should call these vendors for demonstration copies, because much of the usefulness of a computer program depends on how you feel about it. Is it comfortable to you? If not, don't buy it.

If you want more powerful programs that handle tasks separately, you can find many. Prices for the programs below range from $30 to $200. You will pay a higher price from a software store, but you should get some advice along with that. If you don't need the advice, order from a catalog and save your money.

For database management and word processing I recommend **Q&A** by Symantec. It is reasonably priced, not difficult to use, and it combines two programs that are usefully combined. You can do "mail-merge" letters with your guest lists. This function prints out customized letters in short order. You can also print mailing labels or envelopes. This can save you a lot of time if you keep up your database. The computer can store copies of letters you send. This will tell you what guest has received what kind of letter or information.

You can also use Q&A to design and print customized reservation forms. The word processor in the program is as much as you are likely to need and can even handle relatively simple newsletters.

For bookkeeping, you don't need a complex program. The most widely used is **Quicken,** by Intuit. Next to it is **Money Matters,** and one step above is **One-Write Plus,** both by Great American Software. Inns do not require accrual accounting methods (thank goodness) and don't have stacks of receivables (or payables) to deal with. You're a cash business, and all of these programs handle that nicely. One-Write Plus is a computerized version of the paper-based one-write systems with some nice bells and whistles (like a financial statement instantly available).

One nice thing about both Quicken and Money Matters is that they have payroll modules that you can add as you add employees. Handling payroll is such a royal pain that these programs are really worth it. Neither is expensive, and both are easy to use.

There are some combination programs that work reasonably well, but until recently none of them included bookkeeping. That has been remedied by an interesting version of **Microsoft Works for Windows.** This purports to be all you need to run your small business, and it does come pretty close to doing that for the average small inn. To run it you must have a machine with **Windows 3.1** loaded. I recommend you buy your new machine this way if you like the software. (Get a demonstration, please.) Windows is an evolving system that makes an IBM-compatible machine operate something like an Apple Macintosh. Manufacturers and dealers in IBM-compatible personal computers are more often than not including the configuration in new machines.

As far as the machine itself is concerned, you may choose either an Apple Macintosh or IBM-compatible machine. Macs are fine and have excellent software, including Microsoft Works. They are also more expensive per unit of power. Macs have generally been considered a graphics machine and are the principal choice for graphic artists and people who like word processing programs that use graphics. They are not generally regarded as serious business machines, although there are some good account-ing and tax preparation programs for them. On the other hand, they are simpler to set up and learn. Once you master one program, all the others work the same.

Susan Moehl, of Southmoreland on the Plaza in Kansas City, very much favors the Mac because of its graphics capabilities. It allows her to do specific tailoring of all kinds of promotional messages to market niches easily and economically. If you're more interested in the computer as a marketing device than as a reservations and accounting device, then the Mac might well be your best choice.

IBM-compatibles are cheaper, but you will have to spend some time on setup and configuration, and learning is more difficult. Win-dows is supposed to ease this problem.

Always buy a bit more machine than you think you need. It is typical of innkeepers, as with all small-business people, to buy more powerful software and less powerful hardware than they need. Software just gets more powerful and demanding as time goes on; a barely adequate machine now will be inadequate to improved software in the future. Of course, you might find a combination that you never want to update.

Be careful not to try to do too much with a computer. Because you have the capability, you might be inclined to do more than you should. For example, you could research and enter into a database a list of public relations contacts so that you could print out labels for mass mailings. But it would be cheaper and easier to order the labels from Norm Strasma's *Inn Business Review*. For a mere $25, you can get 375 carefully selected contacts and save yourself a lot of time and trouble.

Why you might have to have one some day

Because we do work so hard to make our inns unusual, we lose all the advantages that rigidly controlled chains of hotels and motels have. Guests have a hard time finding us (no single book has everyone) and they don't quite know what to expect. We don't yet have any well-known national reservation service, and travel agents haven't exactly promoted us enthusiastically.

There are budding reservation services that are attempting to link up travel agents, travelers, reservation service organizations, and inns. These services have worked hard with less-than-perfect results, but it doesn't take much to see that this will one day be essential. To participate in these services, you may not need the computer as we know it (we rather hope not), but some kind of chip is going to be driving some kind of reservation system, and we'll all be grateful.

How would it work? Well, it would probably link you through a fiber-optic network to the other participants in the service. It will be possible for travel agents to view a video of your inn, discuss it with you and a client at the same time, and make a booking. Of course, it may be that we'll be able to cut out the middleman, but I doubt it.

In such a future (and it is at least seven to ten years down the road), you'll probably be talking to your computer. And it will probably answer back.

Then our comfortable, old-fashioned hospitality will be more in demand than ever.

A FEW OTHER WAYS TO MAKE MONEY

Besides a restaurant—and there are some doubts that these are real money-makers—there are a few ways to bring additional money into the inn.

Many innkeepers left other careers in order to do what they liked with their time, but all those hard-learned skills need not go to waste. Many of us liked our earlier careers (but not the nine-to-five part), so why leave them behind entirely?

Take advantage of your previous profession. Try consulting or some other extension of what you used to do. If you wish, you can run both income and expenses through your inn; because you're an employee, all the money you make goes to the inn and all your expenses are covered. This can be an efficient use of your time if you can bring in more money through your sideline than you would spend to have someone else do some chore around the inn that you would otherwise do yourself.

Another useful way to bring money in is to have a shop in the inn or attached to it. Small items, from soaps to antiques to travel books, can net enough to make it worth doing. Of course, you have to be a capable buyer. You can also work out arrangements with local craftspeople, farmers, and so on, to stock parts of your shop on consignment. You can include items that you make or bake yourself; cookies go over nicely, as do your home-made breads and jams. Spend a little time at a local crafts fair, and you'll quickly see what is available. Many of your guests will look for souvenirs; postcards and sketches (framed or not) of the inn are good to have. The list can go on and on.

Most successful shopkeepers say that in order to make it work, the shop has to have a clearly marked place of its own. Then you need to notify your guests (and others) that it is available, either through your brochure or your guest letter, or in your opening spiel. A shop can be a relatively cost-effective way of bringing in money, and if it doesn't work, you can always find a use for that space.

One thing we do not approve of is price tags on all the furnishings. Giving guests the impression that they are staying in the middle of a furniture sales floor is not conducive to the friendly, homey atmosphere you are trying to create.

EMPLOYEES

When you do add employees, you can count on having problems. Not all of them are serious problems, but having employees will require more of your time and attention. That means other aspects of your inn will get less. Since your primary job is providing personal service, any diversion is a problem.

Owners who are not ready to take this step can do irreparable harm to their inns. They tend to interfere constantly in the work of those they hire. They refuse to delegate responsibility as well as tasks. And they never believe anyone else can do it as well as they do. With some of the people you hire, that may be true. Few chambermaids will care as you do about the cleanliness of rooms. Few of them will work as quickly as you do. If you find one who does, hold on to that treasure.

Rather than hiring chambermaids, you might try using a professional cleaning service. You have to be prepared to step in if the service doesn't show, but you can more easily say to the owner that a certain worker just isn't right for your inn. Such services don't exist for assistant innkeepers and inn-sitters, however, so you'll probably have to deal with employees anyway.

Very little in handling employees is free of legal constraints. Beause governments often measure the size and success of your company by the number of people you hire, and because most of their taxes come from workers with jobs, all government entities will be deeply interested whenever you hire.

When you do hire, especially for positions that require some thought, you should write job descriptions. That's a service to you and to your potential employees. Your job descriptions can be centered on responsibilities or on specific duties or both. They should be precise enough that anyone with reasonable qualifications can look at the description and know fairly well what needs to be done. Don't be too restrictive in your descriptions. You don't want to mismanage your employees or you'll kill initiative.

If you're hiring an assistant innkeeper, initiative is important. You have to make clear from the start, however, that your inn is yours, and that everything must be done in keeping (excuse the pun) with the personality you have created for it. If you let a strong-willed assistant impose her own taste or methods where you prefer your own, you will have added a headache rather than a helper.

Working with people

A good boss is hard to find. It isn't that most bosses want to be difficult; it's that they are uncomfortable, they don't know how to be better, or they really think they're good when they aren't.

You need to be a good boss. If you aren't, your associates won't work well or together; you, your employees, and your guests will end up unhappy. Guests regard everyone who works in the inn as being there for them. When a guest wants ice, she'll ask the chambermaid, and it won't do to have the request greeted with "That ain't my job," "I dunno," or "Huh?" Train all your employees to understand that the guests come first—within the limits of the house rules.

Training is constant. It has to be constant because you will yourself learn something new nearly every day you're an inn owner. As you learn new things you'll want to pass them on to your staff.

You need to see and talk to your employees often. If you don't, they'll think something is wrong and wonder what they've done. In fact, any sudden change in your usual behavior is liable to set off speculation. You also need to explain, re-explain, and reinforce the policies and procedures you have established for your guests' happiness. Depending on the size of your operation, you may want to have formal meetings once a week. Or, if you have only a few employees, a brief chat in the kitchen at the start of the work day may suffice.

If you have a partner, you should not disagree with one another in front of employees. If one of you says something the other dislikes, bring it up in private, come to an agreement, and follow through with what you agreed on.

If you have a particular way you want things done by the chambermaids, explain first, then check after the first few times the work is done. You should be quick to praise and equally quick to point out errors. But don't micromanage; a white-glove inspection every time a room is cleaned will probably lose you a lot of workers.

Try to make your employees into partners of sorts (they might be some day, if you sell the place to them over time). Encourage them to solve problems with guests, and give them the same right to make mistakes as you gave yourself. You should expect good work from them, and you should expect them to serve your guests well. But remember, you are the final authority. If a room isn't properly cleaned, you're going to hear about it. If a new desk clerk overbooks, you're going to have to pay to put the guest somewhere else.

Some legal considerations

Governments take an interest in your relationships with your employees. Chances are you'll never hear from them, but you might. The best thing you can do for your business is to know where problem areas are and make sure you're operating properly in those areas.

You must give every applicant the same chance to be hired. You may not give different exams or interview questions to different candidates. (In fact, you would be wise not to use an employment test at all, since so many are considered discriminatory.) All candidates must be judged on the same grounds. Do not discriminate against any candidate on the grounds of sex, race, religion, national origin, age, or sexual preference. If you disappoint a candidate and he or she is able to show a pattern of discrimination in hiring, you may find yourself the object of an Equal Employment Opportunity Commission inquiry. The same cautions apply to promotions and compensation.

In an interview or job application form, you will be in trouble if you ask about things such as a candidate's age or marital status. Those questions could be discriminatory. You can't ask about credit ratings or arrest records. You can ask about criminal convictions, although you have to be careful then that you ask *every* candidate the question. You can't require high school graduation unless that is clearly necessary for someone to do the job.

If someone is disabled in some obvious way, you may not discriminate just because you think they can't do the job. For example, if a person is confined to a wheelchair, you can legitimately say that they're not going to be able to clean rooms in your inn, because you have two floors and no elevator. You may not assume that simply because a person is in a wheelchair he or she can't clean rooms (you would be wrong). Further, someone in a wheelchair might make an excellent desk clerk. Think about what the job requires and let that, not their disabilities, guide you.

Background checks can also get you into trouble if you use them to find out about matters not included on an application form. You should check those things that the candidate does put down. A simple phone call to a high school or college to check on graduation will tell you at least that you have an honest person.

Since employers can be sued if they give an unfavorable recommendation of a former employee, you may have a great deal of trouble getting an honest evaluation. Some companies now prohibit managers from giving out any information about a former employee (even the very best ones) except that the person did work for the company and was paid at a certain level. Of course, you may end up talking to someone who will tell you the truth anyway, but don't count on it. For these reasons, recommendation letters and references are growing increasingly worthless.

You need to make sure that you have not hired an illegal alien. Regulations in this area are subject to change. To find out the latest on hiring questions related to immigration law, call the Immigration and Naturalization Service at (202) 535-0170.

Wage scales have to be fair and cannot be below the minimum

wage. There are some exceptions for certain occupations and age groups. This area, too, changes fairly often. For the latest, you can call the Department of Labor, (202) 523-7043.

Benefits are an exceptionally tough area. You will have to pay unemployment tax, Social Security tax (7.5 percent of your employee's net salary, at this writing), and your state's worker's compensation insurance. But you may wish to offer other benefits. If you can afford to, it's an excellent idea, as it helps to attract better help. The first benefit offered is usually paid vacation, followed by health benefits and then by retirement programs. But usually only large operations with steady, growing business can manage this.

Many federal laws and regulations do not apply to very small companies (usually under ten employees), but you can't count on that. There are state laws—often more restrictive—that will regulate employee treatment in companies with as few as three employees.

If all fails and you make a bad hire, you need to correct the error as soon as possible. Document each instance of unacceptable performance (include date, incident, and reason). Vague reasons, such as "She doesn't get along with others," will never hold up as grounds for firing.

Observing these legal niceties is important. Unfair discharge or hiring suits can drain your company and you. And once you are into a suit, nothing except consistently good records and practices will help you.

INSURANCE

You need to have adequate coverage for your business. A homeowner's policy is not sufficient to protect you.

The good news is that most inn-goers are not the types to sue. Nevertheless, accidents happen, and we live in a litigious nation. It would be foolish not to have at least a one-million-dollar liability policy and appropriate loss coverage in case of fire or other disaster. After all, this is more than just a business; usually all your furnishings and home equity are involved.

You may have a separate tenants' policy to cover your personal belongings, although many newer policies cover them along with those of the inn.

There are a number of ancillary policies and riders, all of which can be tailored to your particular situation. You need to find a good agent who understands inns; most agents do not. Your local State Farm rep is pretty good for auto insurance, but he will not insure inns.

9

Don't Forget the Guests

"WHAT A GREAT JOB! A GUEST PAYS TO STAY IN MY
HOME, GIVES ME A LITTLE GIFT BEFORE DEPARTING, AND
THEN SENDS ME A HAND-WRITTEN THANK-YOU CARD FOR MY
HOSPITALITY!"

—Richard Butkus

All innkeepers will agree that the most fun—and most trials—of this business involve guests. But that's as it should be, isn't it? After all, you became an innkeeper so that you could serve your guests.

You already have in mind who those guests will be, and you have created your inn for them. Your success as an innkeeper depends on what they think of you. That means you have to know (or learn) how to anticipate needs and how to do exactly what the guest expects—even before the guest expects it.

On the one hand, you'll find that guests are demanding, even without intending to be. On the other, you'll find that they can be surprisingly tolerant, willing to put up with almost anything to make you feel better. Some guests will be so obnoxious you never want to see them again; others you will want to keep for friends.

But you're also expecting them to pay. And they're expecting you to serve them.

A delicate relationship, that.

"Seacrest Manor is like heaven. Booked for one night and

stayed seven." What prompts a guest to write such a comment? Leighton Saville says, "We have offered a consistently high level of service to our houseguests for each and every day since opening." Business partner Dwight MacCormack agrees: "We don't allow wedding parties at our inn, even though we have the facilities, because of the noise and other factors. We have turned away midweek and off-season business because of this rule, but we feel we must stick to our guns in order to be fair to our clientele who want peace and quiet." They both agree that treating their inn guests "with the same respect and attention one would give a family friend in their own home" is the most effective way to build strong repeat business.

You need to go the extra mile with your guests, not only because you like to, nor because they are paying you, but also because they are two of the three major sources of additional business for you: repeats and referrals.

Being a host, especially a paid host, is not an easy job. Yes, your inn is your stage, but you don't belong at the center of it all the time. The best host is unobtrusive—there when the guests want her, but not if they don't.

This is a hard lesson for most of us. One of the very best things about innkeeping is realizing that we can tell all our tired stories over and over again. Guests are *new victims!* If your stories are good, then perhaps you should be on center stage. On the other hand, most guests are too polite to tell you that they've had enough of you. You have to learn to be quiet without being asked.

As you set your policies, be aware that you must balance your business needs with your guests' needs. That requires flexibility in delicate situations. Ask yourself if it is possible to create a win-win outcome when there is an unhappy guest.

You also have to balance the needs of your various guests. Sometimes the demands of one will cause you to be less hospitable to the others. There are ways to deal with most of these situations, but something new always seems to come up. One of the most frequent comments innkeepers make is "You'd think after seven (or three or ten) years in this business, you would have seen everything. But guests will always surprise you."

We obviously can't tell you everything about dealing with guests, but we can give you some hints for how to handle situations guaranteed to come up. Some problems can be handled by your established policies, but many solutions depend on your style and your ability to think on your feet. Innkeepers have to learn to roll with the punches. Less flexibility than that will surely drive you mad.

AT THE FRONT DOOR

Your welcome sets the whole tone for a guest's visit. It's possible to recover from a disastrous greeting, but it takes more work than doing it right at the start.

Michael Barrier, a colleague, writer about inns, and frequent inn-goer, says, "Because an inn is so much more homelike than a hotel, guests are much more likely to feel as if they are intruding if the innkeeper's greeting is not warm."

We ought not to have to say this, but we will: Your inn is a public accommodation by law. You cannot ignore federal and state civil rights laws protecting citizens from discrimination because of age, race, sexual orientation, creed, or national origin.

If you have any personal prejudices, it is illegal to bring them into your business. If someone whom you have a prejudice against comes to your door, you owe them the same warm welcome any other guest would get. If you cannot do this, find another business.

Sometimes innkeepers have trouble maintaining warmth at greeting—especially if they've just seen the arriving guest drive over a newly planted flower bed. Or, if the first words out of a guest's mouth are, "Your beds better be comfortable, because I have a bad back." You have to bite your tongue to keep from answering, "Actually, it's not your back that's bad, it's your attitude."

The best way to greet your guests is to smile, say "Welcome to the inn," and tell them your name and who you are. Many are first-timers and really don't know quite what to expect. Most people are used to being able to push open the lobby door of a motel or hotel. They are not accustomed to finding the door locked (as a B&B most often is), and having to ring a bell to enter. They're also not always accustomed to being greeted by the owner and may expect a clerk (alas, some travelers do not treat clerks as well as they would an owner).

Darlene McNeill says one of the highest compliments that an innkeeper can give is not to look harried or pressured when the guest arrives. She may have a scrub brush behind the door, but in front of the door she has a smile.

Annette King agrees, and says, "If you look sloppy, with dirty sneakers and mussed hair, then you'll likely get sloppy guests.

They may think they have permission to be careless with your home."

To bear this out: I remember with pleasure a couple of our first guests (they have subsequently returned every year), who drove up in a Jaguar. I was riding our brand-new tractor-mower, wearing jeans and a lumberjack shirt. Without thinking, I hopped off the mower, grabbed up their luggage and took it into the house, invited them to sign the register, and then showed them to their room. Whereupon the gentleman tried to tip me two dollars! At least it was a warm greeting.

I am often in quite casual dress when guests arrive. My reasoning is that the house is so formal that we need a few touches to tone down the formality and make it feel more homey. That's our way. This brings us back to the point that innkeeper and inn together create the ambience. You can't have one without the other.

If your building lends itself to a tour, by all means do one when the guests arrive. They don't always want one; and if not, don't force it. But most guests do. Even if you don't have an unusual or historic building, you should show guests where the common room is and any other little facts they should know, like where breakfast is served and when, where the telephone or the TV set or hot tub is, or where they should or should not walk.

Some inns handle these details by putting a "room letter" in the room. The Inn at Twin Linden gives guests a chatty room letter that tells them useful bits of information like where to get ice, which doors to use, where the hot tub is (and who should not use it), and so on. Writing these details down is often more effective than simply reciting them. People do forget, especially when they are trying to take in so much.

One important piece of information that should be given to every guest on arrival is how to find the innkeeper should that be necessary. Emergencies do occur. If you aren't resident and don't have a resident manager, then you should be quickly available by telephone. If you are resident, let guests know on what door to knock if they can't seem to get any hot water, or if they would like to borrow an ironing board, or if they have a bottle of wine to chill. Make it easy for guests to find you if they need to.

You should also make clear to guests how you do breakfast. This is not standard from inn to inn (and should not be). Some inns do continental whenever the guests like; some have guests sign up for different serving times; some serve all guests at the same time. Most serve the same thing to all guests, but some do have menus.

If you serve the same menu to all guests, you need to find out if any guests have food allergies or restrictions. You may not be able to please everyone (wheat and dairy allergies are especially difficult to accommodate at breakfast), but you should have some simple, handy alternatives. In any case, make sure your guests know how breakfast is done. It is, after all, a major component of your business's name.

Finally, before your guests move off to their rooms you need to make the kinds of offers that will show them you are thinking of them: Do they need a dinner reservation? Would they like any information about what to do in the area? Do they need directions anywhere? Would they like some tea or lemonade and cookies? Nancie and Lee Cabana of Brookview Manor Inn offer newly arrived guests their own copies of a map of the hiking trail that leads to a nearby waterfall. Maryanne Young and Susan Poole of Applewood Manor in Ashville, North Carolina, give out copies of printed directions to Biltmore House, the most popular area attraction. Most inns offer menus of area restaurants, brochures to attractions and shopping, and sometimes even tickets to special events.

HANDLING GROUPS

Inns are becoming popular places for—and are promoting themselves as—locations for small meetings, weddings, and parties. Of these, weddings are the most trying, followed by small meetings, then parties. If you want to take one these functions, by all means do so, but be aware of what you're getting into.

Special events can be a good source of income for inns, but they require a great deal more thought than you would imagine. Many people think they know how to throw a party, but very few really do.

Weddings

Why are weddings the worst? Much of it has to do with the stress inherent in weddings. It is (or is supposed to be) a once-in-a-lifetime event in the lives of two young people. But tradition dictates that the bride's mother is the party-giver, the bride's father pays the bills and stays out of the way, and the groom's parents have very little to do but show up. Brides and grooms, unless they are very strong-willed, are often left aside.

The best weddings seem to be the ones completely planned by the people being married.

In any case, the traditional wedding is the bride's mother's opportunity to pay back every social obligation she has and to show that she can throw a great party. She rarely knows much about the groom's family or friends and often not much more about her daughter's friends. The bride's father is usually unseen and unheard from, except when he is complaining about the mounting cost.

Into this situation steps the innkeeper, eager to get the business and to please. These two impulses, generous and well-meant though they may be, will often work against the best interests of the inn. If the bride's parents pay for all the rooms to put up the bride's party, then you have a house full of nonpaying guests; this, we assure you, is not good. Nonpaying guests will often take advantage of your hospitality, and you will end up disliking them. They are there to party, and by golly they will.

The bride's mother will try to get you to lower the cost or throw in little extras. If you give in too easily to this kind of pressure, you will end up hating the party, the people, and the inn.

This is true to some degree of all gatherings, but more so of weddings. In order to avoid difficulties, you should set your rules firmly and not depart from them under any circumstances (even—especially—for your own friends and family).

We suggest these rules for innkeepers who want to host weddings or parties.

• Set a firm price you will be happy with. This will encourage you to put out whatever extra effort is called for.

• Establish a payment policy. We suggest making half due on the signing of an agreement and the remainder due the week before the event. If the money isn't in hand, cancel the event and keep the deposit. You may lose business, but you won't lose your shirt.

• List all services you will provide and their prices. Then stick to them. If you have estimated incorrectly, and it costs you money, that's your tough luck. But if the party-giver doesn't live up to the agreement, you have the deposit to fall back on.

• Add a service charge to outside services (flowers, catering, rentals) that you arrange. Your time is worth at least ten percent. Smart party-givers will let you make the arrangements. Smart suppliers will work hard, because you represent repeat business to them and they won't want to risk offending you by not doing a good job. Your one-time party-giver may not get the same quality of service that you can get. Even having explained this to many brides' mothers, I have found that they will still opt to save the ten percent. They have usually been sorry. We have been tempted to refuse to do a wedding for which we do not make all the arrangements, but that seems a bit harsh. It may, however, be something you should consider.

• Insist on an adequate damage deposit, and make sure you check after the event for damage. Submit a written statement of damages and the amount you are withholding from the deposit to cover them.

All this may sound too tough for your traditional notion of innkeeping, but the situation demands it. Explaining your rules at the beginning will be a lifesaver for you. If anything goes wrong from that point, it's your own fault. You'll learn quickly from your mistakes.

Business meetings

You should not do meetings unless you are doing them for overnight guests. Otherwise your regular guests will be disturbed. You can't charge enough to make up for that aggravation. But business meetings are good business; one good meeting usually brings you more.

Business meetings have special requirements. Sometimes businesses will have their own meeting planners to take care of these, but small ones will depend on you to do that work.

You need to have a quiet place for the meeting, with good chairs and a table around which all the participants can sit. You can rent appropriate tables if you don't own them, but be sure you include the rental in the charge. If you want to do it right, you will provide notepads and pens or pencils (all with your inn's name printed on them).

Business meetings, if they go all day, generally start around 8:30 to 9 A.M., with coffee and possibly some pastries. There are usually two breaks, one at 10:30 and the other at 2:30, with lunch in between. You should serve coffee and soft drinks at the breaks. All these extras should be quoted in the price you negotiate; do not just throw them in. That's bad business and is not expected.

Business meetings, though they may seem quiet, can drive you nuts. You have to take care of all those breaks and deal with the usual innkeeping requirements at the same time. There will often be requests for photocopying, faxing, telephone calls, and more. You may find yourself being used as a secretary.

If you do it all cheerfully, you will probably get repeat business and referrals.

Retreats

Retreats are popular with many groups, from religious and non-profit organizations to businesses. They combine the overnight stay with meetings, and are therefore excellent business for inns—if you have enough rooms for them.

One advantage you offer to those planning retreats (especially business retreats) is that you can be an activities director for spouses who are brought along but have nothing to do. If you do a good job of entertaining the spouses, they will want to come back for vacations.

Retreats can try your patience. On more than one occasion I have seen a group lose its maturity. For some reason, otherwise sober and dignified people revert to teenage behavior when they are put together in an old house where everything is taken care of for them. It is therefore important to make the rules clear and be prepared to be (on occasion) a rather stern scoutmaster.

DEALING WITH DIFFICULT GUESTS

We all hate to admit it, but there are indeed guests who try your patience. There are even a few (a very few) guests who make you wish you had never become an innkeeper. Because we are generally such optimists, we think this will never happen to us. We assume we're somehow going to be exempt from painful experiences with guests.

Not true, as everyone learns within the first few months. The traveling public is sensitive about costs, and with some rather unpleasant exposés out about the bad bargains some B&Bs are, there will be guests who arrive with chips on their shoulders. And we do sometimes make errors, which puts us in bad with guests, who then act pettishly. Here, we're just going to talk about the difficult guests.

The sourpusses

They can't be pleased. These guests arrive ready to complain. They will dislike something, and sometimes everything. And they will tell you.

Alas, sometimes they are right. If more than one guest complains about the same thing, then you'd better look into it. It may in fact be too cold in that room, or there may be a problem with the water pressure, or there may be too much noise from the next room. Sometimes complainers do you a favor by notifying you of a problem.

I'll never forget one doctor who walked in the door and demanded to know if we had water beds (we don't). He said he had a bad back and couldn't sleep well without one. I smiled and said that we tried to have excellent beds because many guests have sensitive backs, but that we couldn't guarantee more than that. He and his wife stayed, and he complained bitterly the next morning that the birds had awakened him. From that I assumed he had in fact slept well.

The critics

They compare you (unfavorably) with other inns. It doesn't make you happy to have someone tell you that the breakfast they had at Cozy Corners was so much nicer than yours. "They had such nice jams there." The critics will say, "You ought to find out what they have and get some." Do not dump jam on their heads. Smile and tell them you'll certainly inquire about it; letting guests feel superior is one of the pleasures you can afford them. And you might in fact find the jam at Cozy Corners is rather special. We do tend to be thin-skinned about our places. There are lessons to be learned from other inns, and we don't get out to see them as much as we'd like.

The most tempting response to this kind of guest is: "If you're so damn good at this, why don't you open an inn?" Think it, but don't say it. The business doesn't need an innkeeper like him.

Jane Davis, Annette King's sister and budding inn-sitter, told Annette after dealing with some trying guests, "Now I understand why you talk to yourself so much. You're always saying under your breath the things you can't say to the guests."

The freebies

They're not paying, but it'd better be right. For some reason, the most complaints seem to come from people who even have a free or reduced rate for the night. We simply find these folks mysterious. You donate a night to a worthy cause. Someone buys it and gives the night to someone else. The someone else comes, takes one look at the room, and says it isn't what they wanted (or thought it was, or whatever).

Cheerfully change the room (if you have another room to offer). It just isn't worth the lining of your stomach to listen to the whining. Usually such a change satisfies them. Never refund the money—some of them are angling for that.

When the person who has won, purchased, or received a gift certificate for a free night tries to get a "refund," you might be so astonished that you won't be able to answer at first. Explain that the person has won or has been given the night in the inn, not the money equivalent. Some innkeepers put "not transferable" or "cannot be exchanged" on their gift certificates to avoid such problems.

Many gift certificates are never redeemed. That's good, but it's also one reason you should include an expiration date on them.

The boors

Some guests simply take over. They don't always break your rules, but they will push the rules to the limit. Publishing your policies and then sticking to them is the best way to deal with this type of guest.

Hospitality is our business, and even when a guest seems rude or overbearing, we try to accommodate. We'll bend as far as we can to make something right or to try to make a guest happy. But we don't believe our guests are always right.

And then there are the other guests to consider. Most of your guests are strangers to one another, and it's important that these strangers get along in your house. This obliges you to be on your guard to weed out problem guests. If an ironclad rule is broken, you must firmly ask the guest to leave or take some other definitive action. As Heinz Haibach of Millstone Inn says, "You cannot let them walk all over you. They must respect you and your house."

If you don't take charge, you can have the same problem Mae McQuade of Split-Pine Farmhouse had early on. "One novice guest broke all the rules except smoking. He came into the TV room within minutes of arrival and changed the channel I was listening to as I pressed some table linens in the kitchen nearby. When I offered to make him some tea or coffee, he insisted on coming into the kitchen. I waffled and moved the serving pieces I had set out for the morning. The other three in the party came down and he joined them in the formal parlor. When I heard him tell them they could bring in their pizza from the car and use my microwave, the most I could manage was to agree to warm the pizza for them, insisting that they would have to eat it in the TV room and not on my white brocade upholstery. Now I have a copy of house rules which cover these points."

One clue to this abominable behavior is that this guest was a novice to B&Bs. Firmness at the outset in this case is best. Letting a new guest have his way fosters bad habits that will follow him to other inns. Do those other innkeepers a favor and put your foot down now.

Pushy guests are just like children who want to see what they can get away with. They know we want to be accommodating. So they push, and we give, and pretty soon, we give more than we want. You sometimes end up furious, as much with yourself as with the guest. If you let your anger out, the pushy guest feels justified in getting angry back. This isn't fair; it's just the way things are.

Margaret Perry of the Thomas Shepherd Inn had some wedding guests who simply took over. Because her dining room does not accommodate the entire house, she asks people to sign up for a time. These guests did, but then did not show up. They asked for coffee in their rooms, at odd hours. On the second morning they said they didn't want breakfast, but then came down and said they did. They smoked inside the house. None of them was courteous. Margaret finally had enough and told them, firmly, that their behavior was unacceptable. They straightened up after that, but they threatened to say bad things about her inn to others.

If this happens to you, one way to look at it is to say to yourself that you wouldn't want them or their friends back again, anyway.

Courtesy is a basic right in an inn. Discourteous guests have to be defused or isolated, or they will ruin the atmosphere for others. Ninety-nine percent of our guests are courteous in the extreme. If they're around other people who are not, then we won't be doing our job.

If someone cancels a reservation after the established cancellation date and then tries to get out of paying, that person ought to go on your list of people who will always find the inn full. The reason is not revenge; it's to preserve the ambience of the house by keeping away from the other guests those who might spoil it. At the very least, you're going to resent them. You may think that you cannot afford to turn guests away, but in many ways you can't afford not to.

The unreliables

They show up too early or too late. It's amazing how much this disturbs innkeepers. When you're new to the business, you think it doesn't matter when people arrive. Not true. You have many errands to run and much preparation to do, and it is just not conducive to a good experience for you or your guests to have someone arrive in the midst of confusion.

Many innkeepers will not show their inns to casual lookers if the rooms are not made up; we are among them. It just doesn't look good to have vacuum hoses tangled on the floor, or sheets piled high, or cleaning carts sitting out. We all know it has to be done, but it spoils the illusion of the stage if you take the audience behind the scenery. It doesn't matter if the guest says, "Oh, we don't mind if the beds aren't made." You do. And that vacuum cleaner in the hallway may be an insurance liability.

Guests who arrive early should be politely but firmly told that you'll be glad to check them in at the time your brochure states, but before then you are busy preparing the inn so that their visit will be pleasant. They will ask if they can leave their luggage in the room; let them put it in the hall. If you let them in the house, they will want to look around, they will want a glass of water, they will want to use the bathroom, they will want to use the phone . . . Pretty soon, you've lost half an hour.

Even if you have firmly informed your guests of your check-in policies, some people will assume that it's okay if they show up at noon or earlier, or at midnight or later. It isn't malice on their parts, or even spoiled willfulness; they simply don't think.

When this happens to you—and it will—don't lose your temper. Late-arriving guests know they have transgressed. You can still be polite, but firmly inform them that they have broken the rules of the house.

We know of more than one fairly busy inn that locks the doors at 11 P.M. and does not open them for guests arriving after that. In fact, in one, the innkeepers will often book the room to a walk-in at 9 P.M. if they haven't been notified that a guest will be late.

If your stated policies aren't clear, you can't blame the guests for doing as they please.

The weasels

Some guests may try to take advantage of your hospitality. A devious caller may book for two nights, as your minimum stay requires, with no real intention of staying both nights. They will tell you at the breakfast table in the morning that they must depart one day early because of "a death in the family" or "important matters at home." Others will try to use gift certificates or discount offers when they are not valid.

This will make you angry, but with weasels you *must* stand your ground. That's why you have policies—to protect your business interests. Don't accept a transferred gift certificate; don't refund the deposit. If someone "must" leave early, it's the same as if they canceled after your cancellation period: They still owe. And you should collect.

Luckily, the devious guests are few and far between. Keep a fresh perspective and don't punish the next unwitting guest with your leftover hostility.

Innkeepers quickly develop a sense about guests. If a potential guest is inebriated or otherwise not legitimately suited for your establishment, your job is to say politely, "Sorry, no vacancy." You may perhaps even make a referral to a more appropriate nearby motel.

ANSWERS AT THE READY

Have your answers at hand before you are confronted by difficult situations with guests. Most of our problems arise when we are thrown a situation we have not thought about handling. Knowing that these things will happen and having your response prepared will relieve tension for you and for the guests.

Always refer to your policies, and keep them firmly in mind. When your policies are under fire, remember one important fact: *Your inn has rights, and you must defend them.* It is your business and your livelihood. This will give you backbone when it is necessary. The following example shows how to stick to your rules without alienating guests.

Your check-out time is 11 A.M. It is a Monday morning, and you have an empty house that evening. You are looking forward to your first free night in some time.

You have four rooms of guests; three have left by 11. The other couple wants to know if, since there's no one in the house that night, they could check out later—say, three in the afternoon?

Your first reaction is to say yes. But you shouldn't; you will resent it. How do you tell them no without being rude? They are, in a way, paying you a compliment. They are also asking for free time.

Tell them they are welcome to the use of the public spaces and grounds, but that they will have to settle the bill and clear their things out of the room, because you often have walk-ins, and you need to continue on the schedule you have set out. You don't *have* to give them any reasons; you're just being gracious in conceding them that much. Or you can simply say that checkout times are firm, and stick to it.

When it comes to situations like this, think of yourself as the employee of the inn itself: Personify your business, and figure how you would answer to it if you waffled on policy. A partner can serve the same purpose, though it doesn't sound good to say "My husband won't let me do that." That leads to discussions you are better off avoiding.

You do not have to explain why your policies are set as they are. You have thought about them, and you have good reasons for them. You are not depriving any guest of anything that has been promised. The problem comes when you feel you have to take on the manner of a scolding parent to give yourself the backbone to enforce the rules. You don't; just be the friendly, understanding innkeeper who simply says how it is.

Guests *will* understand this. It makes them realize that you are a professionally run business. And that is what you want them to think. You don't have to be rigid, and if you have no problem with making small changes in your rules, then you're being gracious. But if it's a real imposition, then you're just being foolish if you give in.

CORRECTING YOUR MISTAKES

Let's face it. Even the most experienced innkeepers screw up. Nothing feels worse, and we are all inclined to be defensive when we make mistakes. The first rule is this: *always correct the error as quickly and as graciously as possible.*

Overbooking is the most heart-stopping of these errors. It happens at least once to everyone. You're filled for the weekend. A guest shows up, smiling—and they're not in your reservation book. Panic. You should immediately explain the problem and take the fault on yourself, even if it isn't your fault. Find a place, either in your own inn (your own bedroom, sometimes) or, preferably, in an area inn. If the other inn is more expensive, pay for the difference yourself. That creates goodwill.

Sometimes you forget a special request, like ordering roses or champagne for a birthday. Correct it quickly (and hope your florist is sympathetic). Absorb the charge yourself and tell the guest you will do so. Absorbing the charge has a couple of useful effects. One is to make the guest feel a little better. The other is to remind yourself in a painful way not to do it again.

Sometimes you will quote a special rate and forget that you have done so. Leave a space on the reservation card for the rate quoted, and make sure everyone who takes reservations fills that out (especially if you change rates or vary rates during the week). But if the guest informs you that you have overcharged, don't argue. Make a little joke, and charge the amount the guest says.

Sometimes you'll have a guest inform you that her stay is a gift. You should know this when the reservation is taken, and you should indicate on the gift certificate or its accompanying letter that the guest should bring the certificate with them. There are two reasons for this. First, you don't want to have only their word for it (although you should have a corroborating list of gift certificates outstanding to check against). Second, you don't want a used gift certificate hanging around out there for someone else to pick up. Several inns write every gift certificate separately, with the names of the recipients and givers on the certificate.

You do occasionally have problems with smokers, although most now understand that inns limit the practice. If you detect a smoker coming in the door, you ought to make sure he knows you are a nonsmoking inn. You may have forgotten to inform him when the reservations were made. Explain that you may have made an error by not informing him, and ask if he has a problem with that policy. If he does, as courteously as possible find him another room—even if it's at a Sheraton or Holiday Inn.

We all have a responsibility as innkeepers to educate our guests. The effort you make now will save other innkeepers from having the same problems with them.

What constantly charms us is how understanding guests are and how they will often go out of their way not to cause you problems—even when it might be your fault. They understand the fragility of your enterprise and know there are limits to what they can expect. If they like you and your inn, they'll do their best to be pleasant, just as you do.

10

Why You Don't Want to Be in This Alone

We've said before that innkeepers are remarkably helpful about getting other innkeepers started. This is one of the great wonders of the business. Most small-business people are naturally wary about competitors. But in the inn business, although there *are* innkeepers who are jealous of potential competitors, most know that the more people who stay in area inns, the more business there will be for everyone. Under these circumstances, local, state, and national groups, which work for the benefit of all their numbers, have an important role to play in the success of new and established inns.

LOCAL ASSOCIATIONS

Local inn associations have sprung up wherever there is a significant concentration of inns. They serve a number of purposes, and the principal focus of a group will change as the requirements of members and the area change. Focus fluctuates as inns change hands or as innkeepers drop out because they don't find the group useful any more.

Local associations have grown with the innkeeping business. They are now complex organizations with more varied missions than they used to have. You should remember, however, that the association is not the first priority of its members. Everyone has a business to run and possibly even an outside job. Time constraints severely limit what any member can do.

Ray Compton, innkeeper of Spring Bank in Frederick, Maryland, and president of Inns of the Blue Ridge, says good associations do a lot for their members. They can offer joint marketing opportunities, set up member-guest referral systems, share operational business experiences, respond to legislative issues, and establish cooperative purchasing. They can also help prevent innkeepers from becoming isolated.

"Working with other innkeepers in your area is important to create a public awareness of B&Bs," says Peg McCabe of the Queen Anne Inn in Newport, Rhode Island. "On a practical level, local innkeepers help each other with vacancy referral systems. As a group, we try to influence government decisions, like parking restrictions, that may impact inn business."

Associations don't grant membership just because you establish an inn in a given area. Criteria for membership can include complying with local codes; demonstrating concern for guest health and safety; providing a common room for guests to congregate; meeting standards of appearance; and management living on the property. Membership is generally restricted to inns with a maximum of twenty rooms.

Most local associations provide some or all of the following benefits to their members. Each of these can be enormously helpful not only to the new innkeeper but also to the ongoing inn operation that seeks to grow.

Camaraderie

The pioneers of the innkeeping business discovered early on the need to get together and remind themselves that they weren't alone. Innkeepers are generally gregarious people who enjoy groups. But they spend most of their time on stage with guests, who don't really want to hear about problems. Guests, after all, are on holiday. They want to believe that your life is idyllic.

Getting together with other innkeepers allows you to let your hair down and tell war stories. You can describe situations you'd like to know if you've handled well and find out how you might have handled them differently. Often you just have a need to be recognized as something more than just "the innkeeper."

Camaraderie remains basic to such associations, and most require social contact with potential members before they will even consider them for membership. That might seem nitpicking, but it isn't. We've all been in groups with an obstructive member; something about group dynamics seems to require that someone play this role. If a potential new member strikes someone in the group as obnoxious (even if the impression is false), then the group dynamic can be harmed.

Once your local association is established, you can share the common language and experiences that continually revalidate for you your choice of innkeeping as a profession. Greeting and dealing with strangers every day, nice as they are, doesn't substitute for the friendship of like-minded people. All home-based businesses have this problem. Most nine-to-fivers have jobs at which they can rub shoulders with others who share the same problems. Innkeepers need the same kind of sharing, but inns are often widely scattered. Only some effort to plan gatherings can overcome the scheduling difficulties.

Joint marketing

Most members of groups will quickly agree that the major concrete accomplishment of a local association is joint marketing. This usually begins with the group putting out its own brochure. It's hard to overestimate the value of one of these.

Each member can give out the group brochure so it will usually have a wider distribution than any single innkeeper can manage. Groups are often recognized as more legitimate than individual inns (whether or not it's fair) and can sometimes get media coverage that an individual inn, particularly a new one, wouldn't get.

As with all such material, inn-goers and potential inn-goers save these brochures for a long time. Groups often decide not to put prices in group brochures because guests think that a brochure is always current, even if they ought to know otherwise.

The expense of the group brochure is, of course, spread among the member inns. Usually the group can take advantage of the economies of scale not available to individual inns. Groups usually print quite large quantities of these brochures— rarely less than 10,000—and thus can get a good price. It's a great value for members.

Joint advertising has the same advantages. Magazines will give discounts on larger display ads, and members end up getting more exposure than they would as individual inns in the classified section.

Member-guest referral system

At busy times of the year, innkeepers can forget to refer guests on to other inns. More often, we refer them without knowing whether there are rooms available. Local associations can help to smooth out this process.

In the simplest form of referral system, innkeepers take responsibility by turns for keeping up with the availability of rooms in all member inns. Each innkeeper must call in with a status report each week. The central dispatcher then rotates guests needing referrals through the list of inns with rooms available on a given night.

It usually isn't possible for such systems to operate much beyond a week ahead. It also depends on the individual innkeepers to keep the dispatcher up-to-date.

Some groups are more efficient than others at this, and there is clearly a maximum number of inns that can participate effectively. If the group's members are widely spread, it will not always be possible to convince a guest to go 50 miles from their original intended destination. Referrals may not go to the next one up on the list; there is often some attempt to accommodate the guest's preferences for price range, amenities, location, and so on.

It is corrosive to the group for one member to accuse another of being unfair in handing out referrals, so most groups set up rules to prevent unfairness. Most often, however, members police themselves. If you do someone else unfairly, then they will do the same to you. Pretty soon the association will fall apart or the offending member will be invited to leave.

More sophisticated referral systems involve revolving 800 numbers. Telephone technology is such that moving a number from phone to phone is neither difficult nor unreasonably expensive. Inn groups that use this kind of sophisticated telephone or fax system are usually large and in very busy areas. Advances in technology are coming fast and furious, however, and every year brings new and interesting possibilities. With luck, your group will have members who are able to comprehend and adapt such developments for you. And, of course, national professional associations should stay ahead of such developments and help their members, both individuals and groups, to take advantage of them.

Sharing operational experiences

Just as we have shared a good deal of experience from innkeepers across the country, so your group will be a source of advice for those situations that we haven't covered or anticipated. There are a number of region-specific issues that sharing can help focus and solve. You will also continue to need help, particularly in the areas of marketing and promotion.

Group members are usually great at sharing ways of doing things. You're more likely to hear of these at a group meeting. If you feel more comfortable working one-on-one, however, then feel free to call on individuals for advice in particular situations.

Responding to legislative issues

"All politics is local" goes the old politicians' saying, and it is true. When you combine a highly individualistic business like innkeeping with local politics, you have a recipe for frequent, and sometimes acrimonious, political conflict.

Some issues that come up will be local to your community; some will be statewide or national. The most important local issue is usually zoning. Zoning laws and regulations do not hold still; if you are licensed under a zoning exception, that exception can be changed. You may want to oppose or support particular zoning changes around you, and you will need help pressing your opinion in your community. These are highly political situations. City and county councils are made up of fellow citizens with all their virtues and liabilities. They are not above being petty or shortsighted. A strong group will have political impact in those situations.

The other major local or state issues are health regulations—particularly those related to food preparation—and fire codes. Sometimes the enforcement of the regulations is at issue, sometimes the regulations themselves. A third area whose importance is increasing is the levying and distribution of hotel occupancy taxes, usually called "bed tax."

A strong association can help educate decision-makers as to the advantages or disadvantages of regulatory changes affecting your business or community. If your association has (as it should) a political committee, those members should be well informed of looming issues and have recommendations for your group.

If, for example, your association has adopted standards for members and those standards are stricter than the county or state requires, you may wish to press for the official standards to be raised. This will prevent substandard operations from coming into your area and spoiling the image you have established. Such operations will not be able to take advantage of the marketing you have done.

National issues are also important to you, and you can have impact on them. Your senators and representatives are not inaccessible, though you may need advice on how to get to them. Again, there is strength in numbers. Membership in a group will give you better clout and access than you have as an individual. If you are a representative of a business segment like tourism, you are going to get a hearing.

Cooperative purchasing

There's no reason to do more than go to the local supermarket, to buy groceries for an inn of ten rooms or fewer. The same is true for most all of your supplies. If your purchases are minimal, you won't have access to the volume discounts that can save you money. On top of that, there's some value in patronizing local vendors, if you can. How can you ask them for their business if you do not tender them yours?

But if you are larger, or if you can save more than a pittance on large items, then cooperative purchasing can be useful. Most groups don't succeed very well at this because innkeepers don't like to lay out large amounts at one time. Then, too, someone has to accept responsibility for collecting the money and distributing the goods.

There are companies that specialize in working with hotels, and they will provide the same group purchasing power to large inns. They will also do it for a group, if the group presents itself as a single entity. Sometimes this means one inn has to be the "front" inn.

If your group is sufficiently organized to allow this, you can save considerable amounts on large items like refrigerators or vacuum cleaners. You can also save on items that you buy a lot of, such as linens, pillows, and light bulbs.

Establishing standards

This subject will always be touchy for a group, which often is as social as it is professional. We usually find it hard to judge a neighbor, at least to the neighbor's face.

Setting standards is hard. Enforcing them is harder. At some point, however, groups are probably going to have to do this.

They will probably concentrate most on standards that are fairly obvious and easy to get agreement on: cleanliness, adherence to local building and zoning codes, general comfort, presence of commons areas. In other words, the group will insist on certain minimums for membership, in order to give your group marketing some clout.

As far as rigorous standards are concerned, it is unlikely that a local group will take the lead. That has to be done by an outfit with much more distance from each member so that hurt feelings won't cause permanent rifts among neighbors.

Early warning of business problems or opportunities

Local business problems and opportunities should be a major focus of local groups. Working spouses of innkeepers may have connections into area businesses, and the information they gather could be useful for the members of the group.

The sorts of opportunities that come up often appear because your group is organized and known. Inn tours, for example, are quite popular as fund-raisers for charities. They bring in money for the charity, of course, and they get the inns exposed to a wider audience. If you have confidence in your inn, you want as many potential guests as possible to come through. Concentrating them in a given two- or three-day period, you'll avoid the constant hassle of the ringing doorbell.

Other opportunities might involve your group in business promotions for the area. The nature of these promotions depends on the concentration and geographical distribution of inns in your area. If there are fifteen of you in one town, then working with other merchants on a Valentine's Day promotion makes sense.

Business problems for inns often involve politics (see above), but also the potential loss of business. If, for example, there is talk of a major industrial plant leaving town and its departure would cost you a chunk of your business traveler bookings, then you'll want to get your association involved with the Chamber of Commerce, service clubs, and other local businesses to try to persuade that plant to stay.

Disadvantages of groups

If you attended high school, then you know how groups operate. Every group seems to have the same cast of characters. Some members seem obstructive or unnecessarily picky. There are those who want the group to leap into projects without thinking and those who are so tentative that, if they had their way, the group would never get anything done. Some members never voice an opinion and others have an unequivocal position on every issue. Some people in the group will seem to be taking a free ride, never doing their share of the work. Others seem to be in the middle of every project.

All of these behaviors seem reasonable in other contexts. But in an inn group, they can drive you crazy. To your horror, you might even find yourself playing one of these roles. Once you take a position in a group, it's hard to back off, even when you sense you're becoming unreasonable.

Sometimes groups can use an outsider facilitator when they come to an impasse. Sometimes a group will become so divided that members will leave, either voluntarily or by invitation. Shake-ups like this are difficult to deal with, but often lead to a lessening of tension and a new resolve to work together.

One of the most difficult things for a group to handle is the spending of money. Inns operate so often on such a slim margin that innkeepers become naturally parsimonious about any expenditure. Add to that the rather intense independence of inn owners and you have a natural formula for heated debate. We just don't like letting somebody else have a say in how we spend our money. Nevertheless, try to remember the reasons you joined the group to begin with. If you want the benefits of a group brochure, you'll have to throw your fair share in the pot.

STATE AND REGIONAL ASSOCIATIONS

These groups operate much like the local associations, but concentrate more on standards and political issues. They also offer seminars to innkeepers to increase professionalism. The economies of scale offered by a statewide group, whose treasury is often augmented by the state itself, make more ambitious undertakings possible.

State associations are still being formed. Not many are as well organized as the ones in California, Pennsylvania, North Carolina, and Virginia.

The youth of the industry is apparent as these larger organizations struggle to get organized. Innkeepers are very busy and always short of money, so taking two days and spending $200 when the benefits aren't clear tends to cut down on attendance.

But as Sally Palmer, owner of the Palmer House in Oregon, says, "We're not currently working in concert to confront the challenges we face. We need to be able to reach consensus on certain issues. We have a lot of innkeepers who refuse to get involved with the organization because they don't want somebody else to tell them how to run their businesses. I think it's important to have as large and cohesive group as possible. It's the only way we'll be able to deal with these overzealous regulatory bodies."

The larger the group, the more clout it will have with legislative bodies, both state and national.

Another important function of statewide groups is, as Sally says, "to upgrade the image of the business. We have a range of operations in this state that, like the hotel-motel industry, ranges from garbage to luxury. Unfortunately, the traveling public does not know how to differentiate among those accommodations. They go to places without reliable information. We have found that an unhappy B&B customer will generalize his bad experience across the whole industry, whereas a dissatisfied hotel or motel patron will simply avoid that particular establishment. We have had some scathing reviews about poor value. Associations that have an inspection process serve to upgrade the industry. People know they're going to have a nice experience."

Nancy Donaldson at the Old Yacht Club Inn in Santa Barbara, California, has been president of the Southern California Association. She verifies the value of standards. "One of our primary requirements of membership is that the inn be owner-operated. We think that's crucial. The owner must be actively involved with the day-to-day operation and in most cases is living on the premises." Inns must be inspected to become members. "One of the hardest parts is maintaining hospitality. There is a tremendous rate of burnout, and people just get plain tired." To help deal with this the association offers seminars on burnout, one of the most popular seminar subjects of any regional or state association gathering.

NATIONAL AND PROFESSIONAL ASSOCIATIONS

National associations are new to the inn business, and there are just two principal ones: the American Bed & Breakfast Association (AB&BA) and the Professional Association of Innkeepers International (PAII).

PAII exists to professionalize the industry. It publishes a first-rate newsletter, *Innkeeping,* and provides a number of seminars at various locations across the country, surveys of the business, and discounts on services and publications. It is one of the best helps available to the beginning innkeeper. Your membership should begin before you buy your inn.

The AB&BA is more difficult to describe. It publishes guidebooks, keeps statistics on the industry in general, and tries to follow legislation of importance to inns. It has also taken on the role of establishing national standards and in doing so has opened up a wasp's nest.

This is an evolving situation that, at this writing, has only begun to shake out. Because standards are such a hot button for all of us, we'll take an extended look here.

Sarah Sonke, executive director of the AB&BA, says that the association used to publish its guidebooks from descriptions the innkeeper members provided, much like most other guidebooks do. But travelers complained about the value they were receiving, and so she took the association into the previously untouched area of inspections.

"We developed standards over three years with input from members and travelers," she says. The association hired Bill Long, "the biggest gun in the business," and a former evaluator for AAA.

The evaluation program works this way: After you pay your fee to join, you are inspected by an AB&BA inspector. The inspection criteria are spelled out in the association's Quality Assurance Program brochure. The cost for the inspection is partly offset by the annual membership fee. If a member doesn't meet the standards, that inn is not listed in the association's guidebooks. You can imagine the kind of reaction that generates.

Sarah says she gets irritated phone calls and letters from members whose inns have been found lacking, even though they were given time to correct problems. "A certain portion of the membership doesn't pass standards," she says. "Another portion does not believe that anyone should come in and tell them how good or bad they are." But she says her association "had to do this."

To innkeepers worried about the problem of losing their originality and identity, she responds, "People pride themselves on being individual, but after you see a million B&Bs, you can formulate some general characteristics."

To find out what the traveler is looking for, the AB&BA does formal and informal surveys. Complaints by travelers and inspections by her team have convinced her that there are some important reasons why innkeepers lose touch with what travelers really think. She thinks the AB&BA is in a position to bridge the gap.

"Innkeepers always say 'but my guests love me', and that's true. You are the main reason guests come back. They like you, and they won't tell you what's wrong because they hesitate to hurt your feelings. But they will tell us, and that allows us to tell you from a guest's perspective what's right or wrong with your inn."

The most frequent complaint is dirt. She says that many inns are surprisingly substandard in cleanliness and don't even realize it. The second most frequent complaint is the way inns deal with deposits and cancellations. "Most guests don't understand the cancellation policy," she says. "Many innkeepers simply mention their policies during phone calls for reservations. That isn't enough." Unclear or unfair cancellation policies are grounds for losing an AB&BA rating, she says.

"The bottom line is this: Is the inn clean and comfortable, and do guests get their money's worth?" Often they don't. So the first thing she and her inspectors do is ask the rate of each room. Comparing the rate with others in the area tells what the innkeepers think they are providing, from simple accommodations to luxury.

"The rates have to be commensurate with the quality," she says. For the most part, travelers don't see a great number of inns. Only frequent travelers know if they're getting their money's worth. She sees her job as providing perspective to travelers who don't see as many. "We can't put inns in our books if their rates are out of line."

AB&BA also looks at the inn's brochure to check for misleading statements or pictures. Photos can lie or distort.

Innkeepers get a full report and plenty of consultations. They're given a chance to correct problems. If the problems can be corrected before the guidebooks go to press, the inn will be included. "If you pass our minimum standards, then you get a free listing, written by our editors."

Here are some of the things the association requires:

• The area in which the B&B is located must be attractive and safe.

- Convenient parking must be available on or near the premises.
- All interior spaces must meet a high standard of cleanliness.
- Premises must comply with all local, state, and federal fire regulations.
- Guest rooms must have adequate space, storage, heating, and ventilation.
- Beds must be of good quality and in top condition. Bedding must include two sheets, a mattress pad, pillows, pillow cases, and adequate blankets, all in top condition.
- Each guest must be supplied with a large bath towel, hand towel, and washcloth. These must be changed every other day of the guest's stay.
- Each bathroom must be equipped with a commode; combination tub-shower, shower, or tub; sink; adequate shelf space for toiletries; well-illuminated mirror at sink; adequate fixtures for towels; convenient electric outlet; robe hook.
- The inn must have a common room or parlor available during evening and breakfast hours.

Other standards cover breakfast, inn management, security, records, complaint handling, and other important details.

As the industry matures, shortcomings in these areas will hurt everyone. Guests will measure all B&Bs by the one they visit first, so it is in the interests of all innkeepers for marginal ones to disappear.

Innkeepers who have been inspected by the AB&BA, however, have not been uniformly pleased by the experience. Although it will take time, standards will become clearer. But there remains the very real issue of who the association is serving: the traveler or the innkeeper. Sarah Sonke would say she is serving both, but innkeepers are not so sure.

Cynthia La Ferle says, "We need to have standards in this industry. How strident they should be, I haven't decided yet. The AB&BA has some strict rules. Right now, it's an individualized business, but they could make the rules so strict that inns would become as uniform as a Hyatt Regency. If that happens, I'm not so sure it's a good thing. I'm not sure the little details will make or break the inn experience."

You will have to decide if you want to join the AB&BA. Check to see if the circulation of its books will justify it for you. Look at the revised inspection requirements, and be aware that ambience does not rank highly in their process.

OTHER HELP

You can get assistance from joining and working with tourism boards, Chambers of Commerce, and visitor and welcome centers. Not many of them are going to be involved in the specifics of running an inn, but they will help you greatly with marketing and dealing with red tape.

The important thing is that all these groups provide support, advice, comfort, and guidance when you need it. Avoid the temptation to do things in isolation. You have to attend to such a welter of details to run your inn that you can easily neglect the lift you get from working with fellow innkeepers.

Don't go it alone.

---◆---

11

Taking Care of Yourself

"THE WORST DAY AT INNKEEPING IS BETTER THAN THE BEST DAY AT A NINE-TO-FIVE JOB."

—Carl Glassman

If the innkeeper is happy, the enthusiasm is contagious. It spreads to staff and guests, and makes business better.

But, because we spend most of our time thinking about the needs of others, we often neglect ourselves. This is common among caregiving professionals, and innkeepers can get stressed-out in the same way nurses do.

Such work-related stress can have bad consequences for your business. You can become short-tempered with your guests or with your partner (and any innkeeper who says he or she has never been short-tempered is a saint or a liar). You can begin to regard your creation as a monster out to devour you.

You need breaks. But when you're struggling to achieve profitability, especially in the early years, you'll find it hard to close down for several weeks at a time or pay an inn-sitter to keep your doors open. You'll also tend to do what all vacationers do if you do take one: Play too hard.

You also tend to forget your age. Many innkeepers are young, but many more are in at least their middle years. No matter how healthy and energetic you are, you will slow down. You're on your feet and on the go at an instant's notice and at all hours, so you can easily overstress yourself physically. Renovation chores can give you repetitive-motion injuries. Strained backs, pulled ligaments, and the like are not uncommon. And you won't give yourself adequate time to recover.

Sam and Rita Rogers were in their 50s in 1986 when they opened the Melville House in Newport, Rhode Island. They find they are slowing down some. They compensate for it, says Rita, by closing "during the first six weeks of the year, our slowest time, to travel and visit family. We probably lose business in doing so, but it's a lifestyle decision that at our age is important to us, and we're prepared to pay the price."

There is no such thing as paid sick leave. Like other self-employed people, innkeepers typically work unless they literally can't get out of bed. Energetic people find it impossible to sit and rest when there are things to be done—and there are always things to be done in an inn.

To see how easy it is to get burned out, let's go through a "typical" day for an innkeeper—keeping in mind that no two days are ever alike.

A DAY IN THE LIFE

6:30 A.M. Get up, dress, and begin breakfast preparations.

8:30-10:30: Serve breakfast and answer guest questions about what to do and where to go. Check out guests who are leaving. Get cleaning crew (if you have one) started on rooms. Answer calls about reservations.

10:30-12: Make sure all check-outs are done. Write reservation confirmation letters and send out requests for brochures. Make shopping list.

12-1:30: Grab a little lunch. Take some cookies to the welcome center and stop by the Chamber of Commerce to leave more brochures (they're out again).

1:30-2:30: Do the grocery shopping and get back to the inn to freshen up for new guests.

2:30-3: Make sure rooms are ready for new guests and returnees. Meet briefly with a potential supplier making an unannounced sales call.

3-5: Greet new guests and begin setting up for afternoon tea. Make dinner reservations for guests. Bake a batch of cookies. Check the mail for brochure and reservation requests.

5-5:30: Finish setting up for tea. Welcome guests.

5:30-6:30: Serve tea and visit with guests (this is the fun part!).

6:30-7:30: Begin breakfast setup. Eat leftovers from tea—it's your only dinner tonight. Do early preparation for breakfast. Take care of last-minute guest requests.

7:30-9: Attend meeting of downtown merchants' association on proposals for zoning changes. This is an important issue; you agree to be on a committee to study revisions (groan).

9-10:30: Total the day's receipts and prepare deposit slip. Pay bills and set them aside to be mailed. Answer brochure and reservation requests. Call your mother (you forgot to send her a birthday card). Greet guests returning from dinner and see if they need anything. Visit with them a little; this is when they're most relaxed and want to believe you are, too.

10:30-11:30: Take care of last-minute breakfast preparations. Set the table and make sure the dishes you need will be at hand. Check doors and public rooms. Turn off lights and button down. Head for a well-deserved seven hours of rest.

No one day is typical, but they fall into patterns. Try to get on a schedule for paying your bills, maybe once a week or twice a month. Some things ought to be done immediately, like answering reservation and brochure requests—they're your lifeblood. Other things (shopping, we hope) should be once-a-week tasks. We haven't mentioned repairs or any kind of marketing efforts, both of which can be constant.

You can see that with this kind of schedule you'll be tempted to let some things go: exercise ("Climbing the stairs twenty times a day is plenty of exercise"), proper eating habits ("If it's going to go to waste, it might as well go to my waist"), time for yourself ("You mean *I Love Lucy* isn't still on Tuesday nights?"), and time for your family and friends ("I promise I won't miss little Amy's birthday next year").

Somehow you have to make it work for you. If you are lucky enough to have an iron constitution and a saint's disposition, you might be able to keep this up indefinitely. You'll delight in the awestruck reactions of guests who make the mistake of asking what you do all day (I suppose they deserve to be told).

If, however, you're a normal person with a normal tolerance for work, you'll have to do something to stave off burnout. Spend some time thinking about and managing this challenge, just as you do others.

BURNOUT

Burnout means different things to different people. Most describe it as a feeling of being trapped, of working harder and harder to get nowhere, of being short-tempered, of wishing you had yourself and your old life back. This condition slips up on innkeepers, usually about the fourth year. And it happens to the best.

Part of what causes burnout can be poor planning at the beginning and taking on more than you can really manage. But even the best planning can't head off burnout for the innkeepers who want to create a perfect time for every guest. You can really kill yourself trying to do that. Owen often says that I "treat the guests better than their own mothers do." Then I get grouchy when they don't appreciate it.

Too much concern for your guests and not enough for yourself can create burnout. You get to the point where you don't even want to see the guests. You find yourself unable to force yourself to your feet, or you wake up in the middle of the night in tears.

That happened to one of the best and most successful innkeeping couples we know, John and Maureen Magee. For the first two years, they lived across the hall from the front desk. "I woke up crying at 2 A.M. in the second year. I told John, 'You're married to the incredible shrinking innkeeper; all I do is innkeep or sleep.' It turned out that he felt the same way. We sat up all night, and we decided that the only way we could go on was to get out of the inn."

YOUR OWN QUARTERS

The crisis for the Magees worked out well. A neighbor offered them the house next door at an extremely reasonable price, and they bought it for themselves. Things have gone much better for them since.

Some hardy innkeepers manage to live in the middle of all the confusion of running an inn; all of us do to some extent. But the larger and busier your inn, the more important it is for you to create some place of your own away from the craziness. Otherwise, the sense of confinement that is a necessary part of innkeeping will come to seem like prison.

There are ways to create your own quarters, and wise would-be innkeepers will consider this from the start. There may be spare space over the kitchen or a wing you can keep for your own use. Later you might convert that space to rooms, but don't do it at the start. You probably won't need that space at first. And by the time you need additional rooms, you should be able to think about better quarters for yourself.

Some industry observers have said that an inn isn't an inn if the owner-innkeeper doesn't live in it. And some municipalities require the innkeeper to be resident. You therefore have to balance your needs with the requirements of the law. If you live very close by—next door or in another building on the inn property—then in our book you are still resident. If the legal requirement is so strict as to mean the building itself, then you need to create (by adding on, if necessary) truly distinct quarters. You should have one floor or wing to yourself.

Having a place to retreat to, away from your partner as well as your guests, gives you an important sense of sanctuary. Guests will come looking for you, but at least you have that area for your own. Since I'm not at all happy about having people invade my kitchen or office, we instruct the guests to call the inn's number from the guest phone. That way they don't have to come looking for us in a very large building and we don't have to worry about being intruded on when we're feeling grouchy.

Innkeepers with children have to ensure sufficient sleeping and play areas for their families. It's very difficult to run an inn or to raise a family; to do both simultaneously is nearly impossible. Decision point: Hire a nanny to watch the children or an assistant innkeeper to staff the inn. Don't try to do it all yourself.

"After living at the inn for the first seven years, we think having a separate house is wonderful," says Bea Briggs of the Bridgeton Inn in Upper Black Eddy, Pennsylvania. "We no longer have to get far away from the inn to play or to forget the hassles. A separate home has been perfect for raising our two preschool children."

WHAT ABOUT TIME OFF?

You do need time away from your business, and this is hard to manage. If you're lucky, you'll train assistant innkeepers who can be left with the inn. Then you won't have to worry at all (well, maybe a little). Early on, however, you just may not have the cash flow to support a salaried assistant.

This is where inn-sitters come in. Their rates and skills vary greatly, and so will your willingness to trust them. If you can find former innkeepers who have a wanderlust, you're in luck.

You can tell professional inn-sitters by the questions they ask. If they have little curiosity about the house or if they stand quietly listening without taking notes, you probably don't have the right person. A good inn-sitter should want to know as much as possible: how the phone is answered, what your policies are, where you keep the linens, what rooms have what kinds of linens and soaps, what amenities you offer, and on and on. A good inn-sitter will be looking at setting up a long-term relationship with you, so that repeat stays will be that much easier for both of you. This service won't be cheap. You may have to pay a flat rate per day, expenses, and sometimes extra fees for extra work (like making beds and doing laundry). Some inns offer an incentive, perhaps ten percent of gross during the innsitting period, as an encouragement for the inn-sitter to try to keep rooms filled during the engagement.

You could also start an apprenticeship program. Aspiring innkeepers pay you to observe and help at first. As they gain experience, they can take it over by themselves for a week or so at a time. You can then pay them, maybe refunding what they paid you. The advantage to using apprentices is that you have trained these folks to do things your way. And you have seen them work, so you know you can leave your baby with them. The bad part is that you can do this only once with a trainee. If your apprentice is slow in getting her own place, you may be able to leave your inn with her more than once, but this isn't terribly likely.

Once you have the right inn-sitter or apprentice, enjoy your holiday and try not to think about the inn. Sometimes it's a good idea to arrange your vacation so that you can't be tempted to come back early. China may be a bit far, but a vacation in the Caribbean or Hawaii will do wonders for your perspective.

Breaks of at least a week's duration are important; You will relax and find different rhythms in that time. You will also begin to think about your inn in new ways, and fresh ideas and solutions will present themselves.

Of course, you will probably make your vacation an opportunity to get inspiration from other places. Sam Walton, founder of Wal-Mart and one of the most successful retailers in America, loved to go into other stores. He didn't take a large entourage, but he did go through a store with a critical eye. That doesn't mean he wanted to find things wrong; quite the contrary. He was looking for things that his stores could do better. He ignored problems and errors and looked for the good stuff.

When you're out on holiday, you should look at how hospitality is handled elsewhere. And take a tip from Mr. Sam: Look for good stuff you can copy. Away from your inn and its immediate problems, you'll be better able to judge its strengths and weaknesses. This shouldn't contribute to burnout; it should actually revive your original enthusiasm and make your enterprise new for you again.

Just as you schedule maintenance for the inn's buildings, you have to schedule maintenance for yourself. If you don't, the business will suffer. In case you'd forgotten, you're important to its success.

PHYSICAL COMFORTS

It's not just your mental health you have to worry about. Innkeeping is rough on your body as well. Pay attention to the messages your body sends you. Take care of yourself.

Feet

You may think this is a stupid suggestion, but it isn't: *Get several pairs of orthopedic shoes.* Spend the money to get good ones that look fairly good on your feet. You're going to be on them a lot, and if you gain a few extra pounds (almost inevitable), that weight is going to add to the weight on your feet. Furthermore, foot pain becomes leg pain becomes back pain, and all that leads to exhaustion. Most innkeepers say they'd rather have funny-looking footgear than aching feet and backs.

Back

Learn to lift and carry properly. You can make yourself into a beast of burden too easily, and there will come a point when you can do serious permanent injury. Backs suffer especially when you clean bathtubs; the stretch can really cause damage. Here's a little tip: Cut off the handle of a sponge mop about halfway. You can reach to clean a tub without straining your back.

Stomach and heart

You're going to have a lot of food temptations around because you're tempting guests with cookies, breakfast breads, eggs, cheese, puff pastry, and any number of other cholesterol-, sugar-, and fat-rich goodies. Your guests indulge, go away happy, and diet later. You, however, are there all the time. You have to discipline yourself. Consider Ellen Thornber at Llewellyn Lodge in Lexington, Virginia. She gained 50 pounds in her first few years of innkeeping because she ate all the breakfast leftovers. Finally she decided to eat a bowl of cereal in the morning and nothing else; leftovers got dumped. Waste is annoying, but your body has to come first. (Don't feed them to your dog, either. He doesn't need a weight problem any more than you do.)

If you prepare the same thing often enough, you might get sick of it and no longer be tempted. Try to keep some healthy snacks around, for the guests as well as yourself. Your guests will appreciate the gesture and you will be helping yourself as well.

Exercise

You need some physical exertion besides the upstairs-downstairs bed-changing kind. Use your guests as an excuse to invest in an exercise facility, pool, or tennis court. Short of that, get outside and take a vigorous walk three times a week.

Appearance

Your appearance counts for something, not just because of the impression it makes on guests, but also because of the way it makes you feel. You need to treat yourself occasionally to something that makes you look better.

WORKING WITH YOUR PARTNER

Few inns operate as one-person businesses. Those that do quickly acquire a few trusted employees and advisers who often take near-partnership roles.

Couples that work together, make money (and spend and lose it) together, as well as live together can find a whole lot of reasons to get a divorce.

This is especially true when a couple buys an inn so that they can "do something together" to save a strained relationship. Couples have babies for the same reason—and usually with the same result: a quicker breakup.

A strained relationship will get worse by innkeeping. If it isn't strong, innkeeping won't make it stronger. In fact, it will exaggerate those traits in one partner that irritate the other. If one of you is methodical and deliberate, the other may find that maddening in the face of so much to be done. If one of you works quickly, the other may be angered by what seems to be a slapdash and poorly-thought-out job.

Before you take on an inn, a long discussion about yourselves and your relationship is very much in order. A second very long discussion about the roles you will play in this endeavor is also in order.

Most potential innkeeping couples don't do this. They're afraid of what it will turn up. But it is far better to discover these things now than later, because, believe us, your strengths and weaknesses will show up very quickly. Even if you are totally honest with one another and yourselves, you are in for some surprises. You can't always accurately predict what you will actually do and what you are capable of doing (both good and bad).

A good innkeeping experience *can* strengthen a good relationship. It produces a rare intimacy, which in turn fuels the fire of innkeeping. The Southard family—Regina, Jerry and their daughter, Carol—operate the five-room Southard House in Austin, Texas. Jerry sees age and experience as making an easier transition into business. "We were comfortable, very close, happy, and generally predictable as a couple," he says. "Moving three hundred miles and buying the inn was a road of changes that was bumpy at times, but we knew ourselves and each other well. That has made the going easier."

Sid and Judy Clemmer started the Leadville Country Inn with the usual assumptions about who would do what and found themselves wishing that they had been more structured about it.

"I would have insisted—and this is hard for Sid and me—that we define our territories," says Judy. "We operate on totally different levels when we try to do something together. I knew that before we opened the inn, but I kept thinking it would work itself out. If I had it to do over again, I would define my areas and Sid would define his and we would set a meeting time once a week when we would discuss things, but we wouldn't intrude on each other's responsibilities. The way things are now there are constant differences about who has what territory."

They have tended to switch the roles they originally thought they would assume. "She's really the more outgoing of the two of us," Sid says, "and I thought that guest-greeting and all that would be in her area. As it turned out, I'm doing that more and more."

Judy has another interesting observation about the usual partnership arrangement of the small inn, where one partner works outside and the other takes care of the inn. She and Sid are both full-time innkeepers, and theirs is the only partnership in their inn group that does not have one partner working outside the business.

"When one partner holds down a job away from the inn, that person is involved in innkeeping via remote control," Judy says. "They come home in the evening with barbed comments like, 'Why is that spider web up on the ceiling?' The other one, who's been dealing with inn problems all day, just flies off the handle."

These small explosions are very common. It's easy to be critical of things that aren't your responsibility. The partner who works outside the inn may have an easier time than the one who has to live with the inn. Ideally, the inn will begin to make enough money that both partners can be full-time innkeepers, but sometimes that doesn't happen.

Partners need breaks from the inn both together and apart. Both major breaks, where you get out of town altogether, and minor breaks are necessary to avoid burnout. Sometimes the outside partner feels comfortable enough to give the inside partner the weekend, or at least half a day off. Remember, both of you need to get rid of the feeling that you are trapped.

Occasionally, you'll have to compromise with the standards you have set for yourself. You need to let out your resentment against the inn itself. If it is a "person" with its own rights, it can also become a personality capable of driving the innkeepers nuts. Once in a blue moon, leave the key under the mat for late-arriving guests, with directions to their room, and go off to dinner together.

Here are some tips for partners beginning in business:

1. Be honest with each other about your egos, emotions, capabilities, and motivation. Discuss your feelings with your partner. You cannot take shortcuts on these.

2. You have to have one hundred percent faith in one another.

3. Understand that all people have their own needs; be prepared to bite your tongue on the little things. Keep your eye on the main goal.

4. Make a list of what you will be giving up personally—time, money, social life—and make a conscious decision to do so before entering business.

5. If you have children, talk to them about your new ideas. Tell them what you want to do and how it will affect them.

6. Evaluate your finances. Can you afford this? Money woes can destroy relationships.

7. Do you have enough energy? Is your health good enough to stand the work load?

8. Decide that everything you do will be high quality.

9. Give each other space. Keep a sense of humor, especially about yourself.

Sex

We thought about leaving this out, but it's too important. So we've saved the best for last, as it were.

Guests sometimes seem to look at innkeepers the way children look at teachers. They disappeared when they weren't teaching. They certainly didn't have private lives. Maybe they were just kept in the closet between school days.

Guests may come knocking on your door any time. (This is one reason we recommend not showing guests your quarters, but instead giving them a phone number to call.) The long hours and constant disruptions, not to mention heavy business worries, put a real squeeze on innkeepers' sex lives. When we talked to them about it, it turned out to be very much on their minds (and often nowhere else!).

> "It was not her sex appeal," said one man who described himself as a sex-starved single innkeeper, "but the sheer enjoyment with which she devoured the hot buttered croissant that made my pulse begin to quicken."

Most of our informants on this subject, like the innkeeper quoted here, have preferred to remain anonymous. But they were candid.

Innkeepers are only human, and no matter how tidily we divide roles and responsibilities, there is still a tendency to bring problems from the boardroom to the bedroom.

"Taking business duties home (for us a quarter-mile drive) can snuff out any romantic fires that have been set," says Bea Briggs.

Is it possible to keep romantic fires burning while running a successful inn? Says one innkeeper from New Mexico, "Even though we live in a cottage on the inn grounds, it's hard to leave the business and light the candles." She candidly admits that sex is hard when they are under financial stress, "but the love is always there."

Is the entrepreneurial stress innkeepers feel any different from that in any other family-owned, home-based business? "Absolutely," says an innkeeping couple from Michigan. "As inn proprietors, we sleep with all our customers; they don't shop our store for ten minutes, make a purchase, and leave. Nor do we close our business at six o'clock and go home. I can't even get angry and have an argument with my partner for fear a guest would hear us. Both arguments and lovemaking have to be scheduled around this round-the-clock business."

One unabashed innkeeper who always likes to be written about wanted to remain anonymous on this one (it may the only time in his life): "The joy of spontaneous sex is often impossible for an innkeeping couple."

One Minnesota innkeeper argues that residency at the business can present obstacles to intimate relations—particularly during the high season. "Sheer exhaustion from seemingly never-ending sixteen-hour days and the tension of sleeping with one foot on the ground and one ear to the wall can strain even the healthiest relationship."

An Arizona innkeeper who lives with her partner in a suite off the main hallway says, "We tend to collapse, from joy and exhaustion, the first night no guests are registered after a long stretch of full occupancy. Then we run around naked."

Dinie has another perspective on the subject. "I'm a morning person, so I tend to get up first to open the inn and start breakfast. Carl is by nature a night person so he usually has late-night duties. These internal clocks are great for the business, but not the best for *us*. The inn has a life of its own, but so do we. And if we don't schedule time together, it's pretty easy to get trapped at the inn. Time flies whether or not you're having fun."

Other innkeepers had something to say on the subject as well.

From Wyoming: "Birds do it, bees do it—why can't innkeepers do it too?"

From a single innkeeper in Illinois: "I'm not dead from the waist down. Numbed? Yes, but hopefully not permanently!"

From another single innkeeper, this one from Louisiana: "A little flirtation with the guests is acceptable. I'd never cross the line of professionalism and go out socially with a *registered* guest. But, perhaps once he's checked out . . . I enjoy innkeeping very much, but confess that I've fantasized about a knight in shining armor taking me away from all this. Once I catch up with the laundry, I'm okay again."

Who will take care of the caretakers? It *is* possible to keep the romantic fires burning. Some innkeepers "sleep around" in guest rooms at their own inns. Others escape to area hotels for R&R. Whatever your solution, it usually has to be thoughtfully planned.

For dating, the single innkeeper needs to be even better organized. Perhaps it even needs to be deferred until the off-season. In any case, sex and your social life will be scheduled, limited, and quiet.

Comfort yourself with the notion that an awful lot of cheerful hanky-panky is going on around you anyhow, and just join in with some of your own. Inns are *supposed* to be romantic places. As one Delaware innkeeper says, "I don't know how this Victorian frame building keeps from shaking off its foundation with all the rocking going on at my inn."

GETTING OUT

Most innkeepers just keep on ticking. We have met many innkeepers between the ages of 35 and 50 who entered the field in the late 1970s and early 1980s who are still successful and happy innkeepers. It's speculation, of course, but we think that innkeepers are self-selected for endurance. They thrive on the kind of work that would bury most people.

Nevertheless, you will not live forever, and you will probably not be an innkeeper forever. You might as well start thinking now about how you will leave innkeeping so that you can lay the foundation for doing it as you go. We know it seems inappropriate to the romance of the venture to be thinking about this now, but, as with a pre-nuptial agreement, if and when you need it, you'll be glad you made the effort.

As in any growth industry that has experienced rapid expansion over a relatively short period of time, a shakeout may occur. This happens when an oversupply (of rooms, in our case) meets reduced demand. Price wars often result as inns attempt to keep attracting new guests. Discounting of room rates cuts into profits;

some establishments cannot afford it. Undercapitalized inns are particularly vulnerable.

This is the worst situation in which to sell an inn. When there's blood in the water, sharks show up. You're unlikely to get the price you need. Jerry Arndt, insurance agent for innkeepers, has seen this happen to many inns.

"People paid top dollar for inns in New England, thinking the market would never go down," Jerry says. "Then they put a lot of money into their inns—everything they had. In 1991, business was down, they were struggling, and they couldn't sell because they would get less than they had put in." All inns were not doing badly, but the marginal and undercapitalized inns that couldn't afford to wait things out were in deep trouble. "The further south I went," Jerry says, "the happier the innkeepers were."

All of which is to say the normal laws of economics apply to the inn business. Tacky of them, we know. Still, inns seem to have a resiliency. For one thing, they are often innkeepers' homes. For another more and more are opened after the kind of careful research we're recommending to you. We know of very few inns that have declared bankruptcy and closed.

But aside from distress situations, there are good reasons to make a short-term sale. Here are several of them:

1. *The fun is in the flip.* Some inn owners get their kicks from renovating and decorating historic buildings. Others thrive on the challenge of starting a business from scratch. These owners get their satisfaction (and their profits) by selling a turnkey operation. They often run their inns for less than two years.

2. *Lack of money (and energy).* Undercapitalization is the major business cause of short-term sales as well as business failures. We've talked plenty about the reasons for this above.

3. *Lack of understanding of the inn business.* Many inn buyers, not familiar with the nature of the business, discover that their personalities are not suited for innkeeping. We hope that you will have discovered by now if you are right for the job, and that you won't be in this category.

4. *Personal reasons.* Some people fall "inn" love and drag an unwilling spouse along. Such couples are often already having problems, and owning the inn exacerbates them. This may happen even if the inn is successful. There are other personal reasons as well: Changing health or family circumstances (a new baby, perhaps, or an aging parent who needs more care) can be incompatible with innkeeping. Some may miss their old jobs and want to go back to them. Others become lonely and want to move nearer to family and friends. Sometimes people just get an offer too good to refuse.

Sale of a mature business—longer than five years' ownership—is usually the result of personal reasons. Owners who have survived this long have already conquered most financial and business issues. In all likelihood, they have also come to grips with the innkeeping lifestyle and nature of the business. Their reasons might include the following:

1. *Time for retirement.* Many innkeepers entered this business as a second (or third) career and are in their late fifties and early sixties. After five years or more they are ready (and entitled) to a retirement.

2. *Boredom.* Most new innkeepers come into the business with new personal and business goals. These are often achieved after five or seven years. The excitement of building occupancy rates and creating a new life has given way to managing a successful (but steady) business. They sell because they are ready to change careers, or seek new life goals.

3. *Burnout.* Innkeepers who simply can't face repapering the inn or replacing all the linens and draperies or repainting the outside or making a major capital investment that has been deferred are just burned out. They think, "Why sink $30,000 into a new slate roof if we're going to sell the inn soon? We'll never get that money back in the sale price." This kind of thinking means the innkeepers have lost their energy to go on.

Sometimes an innkeeper wants to give up the day-to-day chores of running an inn without losing touch with his baby altogether. One way to do this (and we suspect it will be increasingly used) is to sell to an employee or group of employees. A legal entity is created and an agreement drawn up, so that ownership transfers gradually. This is good for retirement situations, where the owner would like to keep getting income without having to pay huge capital gains taxes.

The devices to accomplish this are complicated and require lawyers and accountants to set up. It may well be worth it, though, particularly if you have built up considerable value in the business.

After they leave the business, innkeepers have a number of

destinations. There is no research in this area, but our interviews have led us to a number of findings.

1. Few go back to their old jobs.

2. Few face financial ruin. Even those innkeepers who had to sell earlier than they planned and who did not yet have a profitable business didn't necessarily face a financial crisis. On the contrary, equity in the real-estate value of the property may even return a short-term capital gain.

3. Some, especially those who are over 60, enter deep retirement.

4. Some become inn-sitters. The need for itinerant innkeepers grows as our industry continues to expand. Many people are full-time professional inn-sitters. Some retired innkeepers go part-time, offering busy innkeepers time off for burnout prevention. Others become regular, part-time employees at their former inns.

5. Many turn avocations into vocations. They pursue new interests they developed while innkeeping—flea marketing, antique dealing, furniture restoration, real-estate sales, crafts, interior decoration, catering. Innkeepers seem to be adaptable, always finding and following new interests. In most cases, their new career paths are as unconventional as innkeeping.

Afterword: Now What?

As we said at the beginning, there's no way we could cover everything having to do with innkeeping. We've tried to give you paths to investigate, rather than a definitive road map.

If, after reading this book, you're still committed to the idea of innkeeping, join The Professional Association of Innkeepers International (PAII), and take a full-scale innkeeping seminar. Then do an apprenticeship. That's the very best advice we can offer you.

THREE VALUABLE OFFERS

To encourage you to do some more investigation, we're making a few offers: First, if you take one of Carl's innkeeping seminars or apprenticeships, he will give you credit for the full price of this book toward your seminar fee.

Second, if you join PAII, you can subtract the cost of this book from the regular membership fee of $150. Write to Professional Association of Innkeepers International, P.O. Box 90710, Santa Barbara, CA 93190. PAII also offers a free aspiring innkeeper's kit containing a sample copy of *Innkeeping* newsletter, "Ten Best Resources" for innkeepers, and "Ten Things to Consider" before buying an inn. Call (805) 569-1853 to receive your free kit or to discuss membership.

Third, on the next page you have a chance to ask a question of the authors.

AND A WORD OF ENCOURAGEMENT

Both of us have stood where you now stand, and we have survived and prospered in this business. You can, too. To those of you who join us, we extend an innkeeper's greeting: Welcome to our house!

---◆---

A Question for the Authors

As part of the price you paid for this book, you may send in a question about your current or proposed inn, and we'll do the best we can to give you a good answer or help you find one.

Please help us out by providing the following information:

Name: _____

Address: _____

_____

Are you a current innkeeper? _____

If yes, how long have you been in business? _____

_____

Are you thinking of starting an inn? _____

If yes, where and when would you like to do so? _____

_____

_____

Your question: _____

_____

_____

_____

_____

Mail this page (no photocopies, please) to either of the authors:

Carl Glassman
Wedgwood Collection of Historic Inns
111 W. Bridge St.
New Hope, PA 18938

Ripley Hotch
The Inn on Montford
296 Montford Ave.
Asheville, NC 28801

Index